PIES

D0053038

by
Jean Paré

Cover Photo

Cranapple Pie page 109

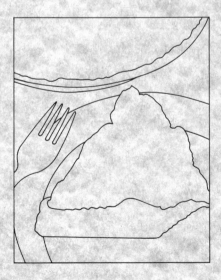

PIES

Fourth Printing February, 1993

ISBN 1-895455-04-9

Published and Distributed by
Company's Coming Publishing Limited
Box 8037, Station "F"
Edmonton, Alberta, Canada
T6H 4N9

**Published Simultaneously in
Canada and the United States of America**

Printed in Canada

Cookbooks in the Company's Coming series by Jean Paré:

English Hard Cover Title

JEAN PARÉ'S FAVORITES
VOLUME ONE

English Soft Cover Titles

150 DELICIOUS SQUARES

CASSEROLES

MUFFINS & MORE

SALADS

APPETIZERS

DESSERTS

SOUPS & SANDWICHES

HOLIDAY ENTERTAINING

COOKIES

VEGETABLES

MAIN COURSES

PASTA

CAKES

BARBECUES

DINNERS OF THE WORLD

LUNCHES

PIES

LIGHT RECIPES (April, 1993)

MICROWAVE COOKING (Sept., 1993)

Cookbooks in the Jean Paré series:

French Soft Cover Titles

150 DÉLICIEUX CARRÉS

LES CASSEROLES

MUFFINS ET PLUS

LES DÎNERS

LES BARBECUES

LES TARTES

DÉLICES DES FÊTES

RECETTES LÉGÈRES (avril 1993)

LES SALADES (mai 1993)

LA CUISSON AU MICRO-ONDES (sept. 199

LES PÂTES (novembre 1993)

table of Contents

The Jean Paré Story 6

Foreword 7

Cakey and Nutty Pies.. 8

Chilled and Chiffon Pies 19

Crustless Pies... 56

Custard and Cream Pies.. 60

Fillings and Toppings.. 77

Frozen Pies 80

Fruit Pies... 93

Meringue Crust Pies 128

Mock Pies 132

Pastry... 138

Tarts 145

Metric Conversion Chart 151

Index 152

Mail Order Coupons 157

the Jean Paré story

Jean Paré was born and raised during the Great Depression in Irma, a small rural town in eastern Alberta, Canada. She grew up understanding that the combination of family, friends and home cooking is the essence of a good life. Jean learned from her mother, Ruby Elford, to appreciate good cooking and was encouraged by her father, Edward Elford, who praised even her earliest attempts. When she left home she took with her many acquired family recipes, her love of cooking and her intriguing desire to read recipe books like novels!

While raising a family of four, Jean was always busy in her kitchen preparing delicious, tasty treats and savory meals for family and friends of all ages. Her reputation flourished as the mom who would happily feed the neighborhood.

In 1963, when her children had all reached school age, Jean volunteered to cater to the 50th anniversary of the Vermilion School of Agriculture, now Lakeland College. Working out of her home, Jean prepared a dinner for over 1000 people which launched a flourishing catering operation that continued for over eighteen years. During that time she was provided with countless opportunities to test new ideas with immediate feedback – resulting in empty plates and contented customers! Whether preparing cocktail sandwiches for a house party or serving a hot meal for 1500 people, Jean Paré earned a reputation for good food, courteous service and reasonable prices.

"Why don't you write a cookbook?" Time and again, as requests for her recipes mounted, Jean was asked that question. Jean's response was to team up with her son Grant Lovig in the fall of 1980 to form Company's Coming Publishing Limited. April 14, 1981 marked the debut of "150 DELICIOUS SQUARES", the first Company's Coming cookbook in what soon would become Canada's most popular cookbook series. Jean released a new title each year for the first six years. The pace quickened and by 1987 the company had begun publishing two titles each year.

Jean Paré's operation has grown from the early days of working out of a spare bedroom in her home to operating a large and fully equipped test kitchen in Vermilion, Alberta, near the home she and her husband Larry built. Full time staff has grown steadily to include marketing personnel located in major cities across Canada plus selected U.S. markets. Home Office is located in Edmonton, Alberta where distribution, accounting and administration functions are headquartered in the company's own recently constructed 20,000 square foot facility. Company's Coming cookbooks are now distributed throughout Canada and the United States plus numerous overseas markets. Translation of the series to the Spanish and French languages began in 1990.

Jean Paré's approach to cooking has always called for easy-to-follow recipes using mostly common, affordable ingredients. Her wonderful collection of time-honored recipes, many of which are family heirlooms, is a welcome addition to any kitchen. That's why we say: taste the tradition.

foreword

Pies. Truly global favorites wherever dessert is enjoyed. What better way to welcome family and friends than with homemade pie? Read on and you will discover more kinds of pies than you ever imagined. Looking for suggestions? Try Osgood Pie, Chocolate Mocha Chiffon or Peach Ice Cream Pie. For a change of pace with fruit, try Pear Pie.

A good pie is a work of art that comes easily! The first step is making a successful crust. Pastry must be handled gently. It is important not to stretch pastry when lining a pie plate or covering a filling. If pastry is stretched it will shrink while baking. Before filling pie shells to be baked, brush with soft margarine or lightly beaten egg white to lessen absorption of liquids. Cook unbaked pastry on the bottom shelf of the oven. Meringue covered pies should be browned near the top third of the oven. If fruit pies or other fillings lack flavor, try adding lemon juice, grated lemon rind, or baking spices. To alter sweetness, make with more or less sugar. Whipped cream dresses up any pie, even if the recipe doesn't call for it. Ice cream makes an excellent topping for pies that are served warm. Meringue toppings are always spectacular. Cheese can be served with any fruit pie but especially with apple. Try it with mincemeat pie and blueberry!

Switching baked pie crusts for another variety can enhance flavors and tempt appetites. For example, a chilled pie may be made in a baked pastry shell, a crumb crust with a graham, vanilla, chocolate or even a peanut butter flavor. To get a golden crust, brush with milk or slightly beaten egg white before baking. If you prefer a golden yellow crust, brush with a mixture of one egg yolk and a tablespoon of water. Sprinkle with granulated sugar for the magic finishing touch.

Pie fillings may be made thicker or thinner by altering the amount of flour, cornstarch or minute tapioca. To catch any potential boil-over in the oven, a pie rack with a hole in the center is very handy to place under a fruit pie. Pies are best served the day they are baked, especially custard or cream pies as they do not freeze very well. Fruit pies freeze well for three to six months, chiffon pies for one month. Baked and unbaked pie shells also freeze very well, easily lasting six months. Most pies will serve six, but extra thick pies or very rich pies will serve at least eight. Whether served as dessert or as a snack day or night, nothing is quite so glorious as a slice of homemade pie. Happy baking!

Jean Paré

JAPANESE FRUIT PIE

Chewy with coconut. Sweet with raisins. A good pie.

Eggs	2	2
Granulated sugar	1 cup	225 mL
Butter or margarine, melted and cooled	1/2 cup	125 mL
Coconut	1/2 cup	125 mL
Raisins	1/2 cup	125 mL
Chopped pecans or walnuts	1/2 cup	125 mL
Vanilla	1 tsp.	5 mL
Vinegar	2 tsp.	10 mL
Unbaked 9 inch (22 cm) pie shell, see page 140	1	1

Beat eggs in mixing bowl until frothy. Beat in sugar and butter.

Add next 5 ingredients. Stir.

Pour into pie shell. Bake on bottom shelf in 350°F (180°C) oven about 40 minutes until set. Yield: 1 pie.

Pictured on page 17.

SHOOFLY PIE

A full pie containing molasses. Economical. Serve warm with ice cream or pouring cream.

All-purpose flour	1 1/4 cups	300 mL
Brown sugar, packed	3/4 cup	175 mL
Salt	1/2 tsp.	2 mL
Butter or margarine	1/2 cup	125 mL
Baking soda	1 tsp.	5 mL
Hot water	1 cup	250 mL
Mild molasses	1/2 cup	125 mL
Egg	1	1
Cinnamon	1/2 tsp.	2 mL
Nutmeg	1/4 tsp.	1 mL
Ginger	1/4 tsp.	1 mL
Unbaked 9 inch (22 cm) pie shell, see page 140	1	1

(continued on next page)

Combine first 4 ingredients in bowl. Cut in butter until crumbly.

Stir baking soda into hot water in another bowl. Add molasses, egg, cinnamon, nutmeg and ginger. Beat.

Sprinkle ⅓ crumb mixture over bottom of pie shell. Pour molasses mixture over top. Sprinkle with remaining crumbs. Bake on bottom shelf in 350°F (180°C) oven about 45 to 50 minutes until a knife inserted in center comes out clean. Yield: 1 pie.

Pictured on page 17.

PECAN CHEESE PIE

The cream cheese, pecan and syrup layers make a good combination. Cheesy good.

FIRST LAYER

Cream cheese, softened	4 oz.	125 g
Granulated sugar	3 tbsp.	50 mL
Egg	1	1
Vanilla	½ tsp.	2 mL
Salt	⅛ tsp.	0.5 mL
Unbaked 9 inch (22 cm) pie shell, see page 140	1	1

SECOND LAYER

Pecans, halves or chopped	¾ cup	175 mL

THIRD LAYER

Eggs	3	3
Granulated sugar	⅓ cup	75 mL
Corn syrup, light or dark	⅔ cup	150 mL
Vanilla	1 tsp.	5 mL

First Layer: Beat cream cheese and sugar together in small mixing bowl until smooth. Add egg, vanilla and salt. Beat at medium speed until smooth.

Pour into pie shell.

Second Layer: Sprinkle pecans over cheese layer.

Third Layer: Beat eggs in small mixing bowl until frothy. Add sugar, syrup and vanilla. Beat slowly until blended. Pour over pecans. Bake in 375°F (190°C) oven about 35 to 40 minutes until set and center feels firm to touch. Yield: 1 pie.

LEMON SPONGE PIE

Soft and lemony. Different from usual lemon pies. Excellent.

Egg whites, room temperature	3	3
Egg yolks	3	3
Butter or margarine, softened	2 tbsp.	30 mL
Grated rind of lemon	1	1
Juice of lemon	1	1
Milk	1 cup	250 mL
Granulated sugar	1 cup	250 mL
All-purpose flour	1/4 cup	60 mL
Salt	1/8 tsp.	0.5 mL
Unbaked 9 inch (22 cm) pie shell, see page 140	1	1

Beat egg whites in small mixing bowl until stiff. Set aside.

In separate bowl beat egg yolks. Slowly beat in butter, lemon rind, lemon juice and milk.

In another small bowl stir sugar, flour and salt. Mix into milk mixture. Fold into egg whites.

Pour into pie shell. Bake on bottom shelf in 350°F (180°C) oven about 35 to 40 minutes until puffy and golden brown. Yield: 1 pie.

LEMON CHESS PIE

From the southern states of North America comes this variation of Chess Pie.

Eggs	4	4
Granulated sugar	2 cups	450 mL
All-purpose flour	1 tbsp.	15 mL
Cornmeal	1 tbsp.	15 mL
Lemon juice	1/4 cup	50 mL
Grated lemon rind	1 tbsp.	15 mL
Milk	1/4 cup	50 mL
Butter or margarine, melted	1/4 cup	50 mL
Unbaked 9 inch (22 cm) pie shell, see page 140	1	1

(continued on next page)

Beat eggs in mixing bowl until frothy.

Add next 7 ingredients. Beat until smooth.

Pour into pie shell. If you are using a store-bought 9 inch (22 cm) pie shell, this will be too much filling. Cook about ²/₃ cup (150 mL) filling separately in small bowl. Bake in 350°F (180°C) oven for 40 to 50 minutes until set and browned well on top. Yield: 1 pie.

OSGOOD PIE

A raisin and pecan cross. One of the best.

Butter or margarine, softened	¹/₂ cup	125 mL
Granulated sugar	1 cup	225 mL
Egg yolks	4	4
Vinegar	1 tsp.	5 mL
Vanilla	1 tsp.	5 mL
Cinnamon	¹/₂ tsp.	2 mL
Allspice	¹/₂ tsp.	2 mL
Raisins	³/₄ cup	175 mL
Pecans, whole or chopped	³/₄ cup	175 mL
Egg whites, room temperature	4	4
Unbaked 9 inch (22 cm) pie shell, see page 140	1	1

Cream butter and sugar together. Beat in egg yolks. Add vinegar, vanilla, cinnamon and allspice. Mix.

Stir in raisins and pecans.

Beat egg whites in bowl until stiff. Fold into pie batter.

Turn into pie shell. Bake on bottom shelf in 350°F (180°C) oven about 35 to 40 minutes until set. Yield: 1 pie.

Paré Pointer

If you have termites and rabbits you have bugs bunnies.

KENTUCKY DERBY PIE

Chocolate chips and nuts - what more could you ask?

Semisweet chocolate chips	1 cup	250 mL
Unbaked 9 inch (22 cm) pie shell, see page 140	1	1
FILLING		
Butter or margarine, melted	1/2 cup	125 mL
Granulated sugar	1 cup	225 mL
Eggs	2	2
Vanilla	1 tsp.	5 mL
Bourbon	2 tbsp.	30 mL
All-purpose flour	1/2 cup	125 mL
Chopped pecans	1 cup	250 mL

Sprinkle chocolate chips over bottom of pie shell.

Filling: Combine butter and sugar in bowl. Cream together well. Add eggs 1 at a time beating well after each addition. Add vanilla and bourbon. Mix.

Stir in flour and pecans. Pour over chocolate chips. Bake in 350°F (180°C) oven about 40 to 50 minutes until an inserted wooden toothpick comes out clean. Yield: 1 pie.

CHOCOLATE PECAN PIE: Simply omit bourbon.

BROWNIE PIE

A cakey filling in a pie shell. Cut pieces small, as pie is rich. Especially delicious with a small scoop of ice cream topped with some chocolate sauce.

Butter or margarine, softened	1/2 cup	125 mL
Granulated sugar	1 cup	250 mL
Cocoa	3 tbsp.	50 mL
Eggs	2	2
Vanilla	1 tsp.	5 mL
All-purpose flour	2/3 cup	150 mL
Chopped walnuts or pecans	1/2 cup	125 mL
Unbaked 9 inch (22 cm) pie shell, see page 140	1	1

(continued on next page)

Combine butter, sugar and cocoa in medium saucepan over medium heat. Stir until butter is melted. Remove from heat.

Beat in eggs 1 at a time. Add vanilla.

Stir in flour and walnuts.

Turn into pie shell. Bake in 350°F (180°C) oven about 30 minutes until set. To test for doneness, an inserted wooden toothpick will come out moist and a bit crumby. Serve warm or cooled. Yield: 1 pie.

TURTLE PIE

Very rich, so small servings suffice. A toffee-like filling between pecans and chocolate.

Chopped pecans	¹/₃ cup	75 mL
Baked 9 inch (22 cm) pie shell, see page 140	1	1
Sweetened condensed milk	¹/₂ cup	125 mL
Brown sugar, packed	¹/₂ cup	125 mL
Butter or margarine	¹/₂ cup	125 mL
Corn syrup	2 tbsp.	30 mL
Pecan halves	16	16
Semisweet chocolate chips	²/₃ cup	150 mL
Butter or margarine	2 tbsp.	30 mL

Sprinkle chopped pecans over bottom of pie shell.

Combine next 4 ingredients in heavy saucepan over medium heat. Stir and bring to a boil. Keep stirring as it continues to boil for 5 minutes. Be careful because it sticks to the bottom of the pan quite readily. Remove from heat. Slowly beat with spoon about 2 minutes until it shows signs of thickening; not too long or it will harden when cool. Carefully spoon over chopped pecans.

Visualize the pie being cut into 8 wedges. Now place pecan halves around outside edge in upright position against crust so there will be 2 in each wedge. These are the turtle's feet. Push them down into filling so they stay upright. Cool.

Melt chocolate chips and butter in small saucepan over low heat. Spread over pie. Chill. Yield: 1 pie.

Pictured on page 71.

BAKEWELL TART

This variation is baked in a pie shell. It also serves as a great filling for tarts. Very good.

Raspberry jam or other red jam	¹/₂ cup	125 mL
Unbaked 9 inch (22 cm) pie shell, see page 140	1	1
FILLING		
Butter or margarine, softened	¹/₂ cup	125 mL
Granulated sugar	¹/₂ cup	125 mL
Egg yolks	3	3
Fine bread crumbs (or dried cake crumbs, rolled fine)	¹/₃ cup	75 mL
Almond flavoring	¹/₄ tsp.	1 mL
Ground almonds	³/₄ cup	175 mL
Egg whites, room temperature	3	3

Spread jam in bottom of pie shell.

Filling: Mix first 6 ingredients in bowl in order given.

Beat egg whites until stiff. Fold into almond mixture. Pour over jam in pie shell. Bake on bottom shelf in 350°F (180°C) oven about 40 minutes until set and feels firm to touch. Yield: 1 pie.

CANDY PECAN PIE

A smooth chocolate filling with lots of nuts.

Semisweet chocolate chips	1 cup	250 mL
Butter or margarine	¹/₄ cup	50 mL
Sweetened condensed milk (see Note)	11 oz.	300 mL
Eggs	2	2
Vanilla	1 tsp.	5 mL
Salt	¹/₈ tsp.	0.5 mL
Pecans, halves or chopped	1 cup	250 mL
Unbaked 9 inch (22 cm) pie shell, see page 140	1	1

(continued on next page)

Combine first 3 ingredients in saucepan over medium heat. Stir often until chocolate chips melt and mixture is smooth. Remove from heat.

Stir in eggs, vanilla and salt.

Add pecans. Mix.

Pour into pie shell. Bake on bottom shelf in 350°F (180°C) oven about 40 to 45 minutes until set. Serve warm or cold. Yield: 1 pie.

Note: A 14 oz. (398 mL) can may also be used.

PECAN PIE

A nutty top with a smooth rich filling.

Eggs	3	3
Granulated or brown sugar	1 cup	250 mL
All-purpose flour	1 tbsp.	15 mL
Corn syrup, light or dark	1 cup	250 mL
Butter or margarine, melted	2 tbsp.	30 mL
Vanilla	1 tsp.	5 mL
Pecan halves, small size if possible	1 cup	250 mL
Unbaked 9 inch (22 cm) pie shell, see page 140	1	1

Beat eggs slightly in bowl. Mix in sugar and flour. Add syrup, butter and vanilla. Stir in pecans.

Pour into pie shell. Bake on bottom shelf in 350°F (180°C) oven about 50 to 60 minutes until center is almost set. A knife inserted half way between center and edge should come out clean. Cool. Yield: 1 pie.

Paré Pointer

It is a wonder Father Time isn't covered with bandages the way day breaks and night falls.

RAISIN NUT PIE

The flavor will remind you of a spice cake.

Granulated sugar	1 cup	225 mL
Egg yolks	3	3
Butter or margarine, softened	2 tbsp.	30 mL
Vinegar	2 tsp.	10 mL
Cinnamon	1/2 tsp.	2 mL
Nutmeg	1/4 tsp.	1 mL
Raisins	1 cup	250 mL
Chopped walnuts or pecans	1/2 cup	125 mL
Egg whites, room temperature	3	3
Unbaked 9 inch (22 cm) pie shell, see page 140	1	1

Combine first 6 ingredients in bowl. Beat well.

Stir in raisins and walnuts.

Beat egg whites in small bowl until stiff. Fold into raisin mixture.

Pour into pie shell. Bake in 350°F (180°C) oven about 30 to 40 minutes until set. Serve warm. Yield: 1 pie.

1. Japanese Fruit Pie page 8
2. Shoofly Pie page 8
3. Coffee Toffee Pie page 26
4. Black Bottom Pie page 64

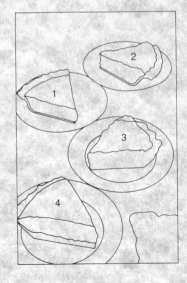

FRENCH COCONUT PIE

A marvelous texture and a just right flavor.

Eggs	3	3
Granulated sugar	1½ cups	350 mL
Butter or margarine, melted	½ cup	125 mL
Lemon juice	1 tbsp.	15 mL
Vanilla	1 tsp.	5 mL
Fine coconut	1 cup	225 mL
Unbaked 9 inch (22 cm) pie shell, see page 140	1	1

Beat eggs in mixing bowl until frothy. Add sugar and butter. Beat. Stir in lemon juice, vanilla and coconut.

Pour into pie shell. Bake on bottom shelf in 350°F (180°C) oven about 40 minutes until set. Yield: 1 pie.

GLAZED CHERRY PIE

Fresh cherries in cherry gelatin. Serve with whipped cream for the finishing touch.

Cherry flavored gelatin (jelly powder)	1 x 3 oz.	1 x 85 g
Boiling water	⅔ cup	150 mL
Granulated sugar	1 cup	250 mL
Fresh cherries, pitted	2 cups	500 mL
Fresh cherries, pitted and halved	2 cups	500 mL
Baked 9 inch (22 cm) pie shell, see page 140	1	1

Stir gelatin into boiling water in medium bowl until dissolved.

Combine sugar and first amount of cherries in medium saucepan. Stir. Mash cherries then heat and stir until it boils. Cook for 2 minutes. Add gelatin mixture. Remove from heat.

Place second amount of cherries in pie shell. Pour hot mixture over top. Just use what pie shell will hold. A bit may need to be left out. Chill at least 4 hours before cutting. Yield: 1 pie.

PUMPKIN PECAN PIE

Pumpkin filling and a nutty topping. The best of both worlds.

Eggs	3	3
Canned pumpkin, without spices	14 oz.	398 mL
Granulated sugar	1/2 cup	125 mL
Corn syrup	1/2 cup	125 mL
Cinnamon	3/4 tsp.	4 mL
Ginger	1/4 tsp.	1 mL
Salt	1/4 tsp.	1 mL
Butter or margarine, melted	2 tbsp.	30 mL
Unbaked 9 inch (22 cm) pie shell, see page 140	1	1
Chopped pecans or walnuts	1 cup	250 mL
Whipped Cream, see page 30		

Beat eggs lightly in mixing bowl. Add and mix next 7 ingredients in order given.

Pour into pie shell.

Sprinkle pecans evenly over top. Bake on bottom rack in 450°F (235°C) oven for 10 minutes. Lower heat to 350°F (180°C) and bake about 35 minutes until a knife inserted close to center comes out clean. Cool.

Serve with dollops of whipped cream. Yield: 1 pie.

PINEAPPLE WINK PIE

Also quick as a wink to make. A touch tart rather than sweet.

Crushed pineapple with juice	14 oz.	398 mL
Sour cream	1 cup	225 mL
Instant vanilla pudding, 4 serving size	1	1
Baked 9 inch (22 cm) pie shell, see page 140	1	1
Whipped Cream, see page 30		

Place first 3 ingredients in bowl. Stir well.

Pour into pie shell. Chill.

Spread with whipped cream. Yield: 1 pie.

RASPBERRY CITRUS PIE

Creamy smooth. Thick wedges that are very good.

Baked Graham Cracker Crust, see page 73	1	1
Sweetened condensed milk (see Note)	11 oz.	300 mL
Lime juice	1/2 cup	125 mL
Frozen whipped topping, thawed	2 cups	500 mL
Drops of red food coloring (optional)	3-6	3-6
Fresh raspberries	1 cup	250 mL
Fresh raspberries	8-12	8-12

Prepare crust. Cool.

Empty condensed milk into bowl. Stir in lime juice. Fold in whipped topping and food coloring.

Carefully fold in first amount of raspberries. Turn into pie shell.

Garnish with remaining raspberries making a little pile in the middle. Chill. Yield: 1 pie.

Note: A 14 oz. (398 mL) can may also be used.

CHILLED BLUEBERRY PIE

You'll argue over who gets the last piece.

Cream cheese, softened	8 oz.	250 g
Icing (confectioner's) sugar	1 cup	250 mL
Lemon juice	1 tbsp.	15 mL
Frozen whipped topping, thawed	2 cups	500 mL
Baked Graham Cracker Crust, see page 73	1	1
Canned blueberry pie filling	19 oz.	540 mL

Beat cream cheese, icing sugar and lemon juice in small bowl until smooth.

Fold whipped topping into cheese mixture.

Pour into pie shell. Chill for about 2 hours.

Spoon pie filling over top. You probably will not need to use the whole can, but lots of topping is always acceptable. Chill. Yield: 1 pie.

LIME CHIFFON PIE

Especially welcome on a summer day, this is good in a pastry crust but is extra special in a chocolate crust.

Unflavored gelatin	1 x ¼ oz.	1 x 7 g
Water	¼ cup	60 mL
Lime juice	½ cup	125 mL
Egg yolks	4	4
Granulated sugar	⅔ cup	150 mL
Finely grated lime rind	1 tsp.	5 mL
Egg whites, room temperature	4	4
Granulated sugar	½ cup	125 mL
Whipping cream (or 1½ envelopes topping)	1½ cups	375 mL
Drops of green food coloring (optional)	2-4	2-4
Baked 9 inch (22 cm) pie shell, see page 140, or Chocolate Cookie Crust, see page 29	1	1
Chocolate curls		
Reserved whipped cream	1 cup	250 mL

Sprinkle gelatin over water in heavy saucepan. Let stand 1 minute. Heat and stir until it boils.

In small bowl combine next 4 ingredients. Beat well with spoon. Stir into boiling gelatin until it returns to a boil. Cool then chill until it mounds when dropped from spoon.

Beat egg whites until a stiff froth. Gradually beat in second amount of sugar until stiff and sugar is dissolved. Fold into thickened mixture.

Beat cream in small bowl until stiff. Reserve 1 cup (250 mL). Fold remaining cream into gelatin mixture. Fold in green food coloring if using.

Pour into pie shell. Chill.

To serve, place a cluster of chocolate curls in center. Pipe border of reserved cream around outside edge. Chill. Yield: 1 pie.

DAIQUIRI PIE: Use only 2 tbsp. (30 mL) water instead of ¼ cup (60 mL). Add 2 to 3 tbsp. (30 to 45 mL) of light rum to water. Go by taste.

CHOCOLATE MOCHA CHIFFON PIE

A large, high pie resembling chocolate mousse. This is a perfect chocolate fix for the day!

Unflavored gelatin	2 x ¼ oz.	2 x 7 g
Water	½ cup	125 mL
Butter or margarine	2 tbsp.	30 mL
Cocoa	½ cup	125 mL
Milk	1¾ cups	400 mL
Granulated sugar	½ cup	125 mL
Instant coffee granules	3 tbsp.	50 mL
Vanilla	1 tsp.	5 mL
Egg yolks	2	2
Egg whites, room temperature	2	2
Cream of tartar	¼ tsp.	1 mL
Granulated sugar	½ cup	125 mL
Whipping cream (or 1 envelope topping)	1 cup	250 mL
Baked 9 inch (22 cm) pie shell, see page 140	1	1
WHIPPED CREAM (optional)		
Whipping cream (or 1 envelope topping)	1 cup	250 mL
Granulated sugar	2 tsp.	10 mL
Vanilla	½ tsp.	2 mL

Sprinkle gelatin over water in medium saucepan. Let stand for 1 minute. Heat and stir to dissolve gelatin.

Add butter, cocoa and milk. Heat, stirring often as it comes to a boil.

In small bowl combine first amount of sugar, coffee granules, vanilla and egg yolks. Mix well. Stir into boiling milk mixture until it returns to a boil. Remove from heat. Chill until it will mound when dropped from spoon.

Beat egg whites and cream of tartar until soft peaks form. Add second amount of sugar slowly, beating until stiff. Fold into chilled mixture.

Beat whipping cream until stiff. Fold into chilled mixture. Turn into pie shell. Chill.

Whipped Cream: In small mixing bowl, beat cream, sugar and vanilla until stiff. Spoon over pie. Yield: 1 pie.

Pictured on page 71.

PINEAPPLE GLORY PIE

A heavenly pie. Pinkish color is from the cherries. Good, thick and juicy with an excellent shortbread crust.

SHORTBREAD CRUST

All-purpose flour	1¹/₂ cups	350 mL
Granulated sugar	2 tbsp.	30 mL
Butter or margarine	³/₄ cup	175 mL

FILLING

Crushed pineapple with juice	19 oz.	540 mL
Granulated sugar	²/₃ cup	150 mL
Cornstarch	3 tbsp.	50 mL
Lemon juice	1 tsp.	5 mL
Chopped maraschino cherries	¹/₃ cup	75 mL
Cherry juice	3¹/₂ tbsp.	55 mL
Almond flavoring	1 tsp.	5 mL

MERINGUE

Egg whites, room temperature	3	3
Cream of tartar	¹/₄ tsp.	1 mL
Granulated sugar	¹/₄ cup	50 mL
Vanilla	1 tsp.	5 mL
Medium coconut	2 tbsp.	30 mL

Shortbread Crust: Mix all 3 ingredients until crumbly. Press onto bottom and sides of 9 inch (22 cm) pie plate. Bake in 350°F (180°C) oven about 15 minutes until lightly browned. Cool.

Filling: Combine first 4 ingredients in saucepan. Mix well to dissolve cornstarch. Stir over medium heat until it boils and thickens. Remove from heat.

Stir in cherries, cherry juice and almond flavoring. Pour into pie shell.

Meringue: Beat egg whites and cream of tartar until a stiff froth. Gradually add sugar, beating until stiff and sugar is dissolved. Add vanilla. Spread over filling pushing to edge of crust to seal all around.

Sprinkle with coconut. Bake in 350°F (180°C) oven about 10 minutes until browned. Cool. Yield: 1 pie.

Pictured on page 107.

A classic that has always been with us. Very light.

Baked Graham Cracker Crust, page 73 or Pastry, page 140	1	1
Unflavored gelatin	1 x ¼ oz.	1 x 7 g
Water	½ cup	125 mL
Granulated sugar	⅔ cup	150 mL
Egg yolks	3	3
Crème de cacao	2 tbsp.	30 mL
Brandy	2 tbsp.	30 mL
Egg whites, room temperature	3	3
Whipping cream (or 1 envelope topping)	1 cup	250 mL
WHIPPED CREAM		
Whipping cream (or 1 envelope topping)	1 cup	250 mL
Icing (confectioner's) sugar	1 tbsp.	15 mL
Chocolate curls		

Prepare crust. Cool.

Sprinkle gelatin over water in small saucepan. Let stand 1 minute. Heat and stir to dissolve gelatin.

Mix sugar and egg yolks in small bowl. Add to gelatin and stir until it starts to boil. Remove from heat.

Add crème de cacao and brandy. Chill until it mounds slightly when spooned over itself.

Beat egg whites in small mixing bowl until stiff. Fold into chilled filling.

Using same beaters and bowl, whip cream until stiff. Fold into filling. Turn into pie shell. Chill.

Whipped Cream: Beat cream and sugar until thick. Spoon onto pie.

Garnish with chocolate curls. Yield: 1 pie.

COFFEE TOFFEE PIE

Indulge! This pie firms overnight. Just finish with topping and you are all set.

CHOCOLATE PIE SHELL

Packaged pie crust mix (1/2 envelope)	1 cup	225 mL
Brown sugar, packed	1/4 cup	50 mL
Ground or finely chopped walnuts	1/2 cup	125 mL
Cocoa	2 tbsp.	30 mL
Water	1 tbsp.	15 mL

FILLING

Butter or margarine, softened	1/2 cup	125 mL
Granulated sugar	3/4 cup	175 mL
Instant coffee granules	2 tsp.	10 mL
Unsweetened baking chocolate square, melted	1 × 1 oz.	1 × 28 g
Eggs	2	2

COFFEE TOPPING

Whipping cream (or 1 envelope topping)	1 cup	250 mL
Icing (confectioner's) sugar	1/4 cup	50 mL
Instant coffee granules, crushed to a powder	1 tbsp.	15 mL

Chocolate curls

Chocolate Pie Shell: Combine all 5 ingredients in bowl. Mix. Roll on floured surface. Line 9 inch (22 cm) pie plate. Bake in 425°F (220°C) oven for 10 minutes. Cool.

Filling: Cream butter and sugar together in small mixing bowl. Mix in coffee granules and chocolate. Add 1 egg and beat for 5 minutes. Add second egg and beat 5 minutes more.

Turn into pie shell. Cover and chill overnight.

Coffee Topping: Beat cream, sugar and crushed coffee together in bowl until stiff. Spread over pie. Chill.

Put chocolate curls on top. Yield: 1 pie.

Pictured on page 17.

PUMPKIN CHIFFON PIE

Beaten egg whites and cream make this a light pie that requires no baking.

Milk	¹/₂ cup	125 mL
Canned pumpkin, without spices	14 oz.	398 mL
Unflavored gelatin	1 × ¹/₄ oz.	1 × 7 g
Water	¹/₄ cup	50 mL
Brown sugar, packed	¹/₂ cup	125 mL
Cinnamon	³/₄ tsp.	4 mL
Ginger	¹/₂ tsp.	2 mL
Nutmeg	¹/₄ tsp.	1 mL
Salt	¹/₄ tsp.	1 mL
Egg yolks	3	3
Egg whites, room temperature	3	3
Granulated sugar	6 tbsp.	100 mL
Whipping cream (or 1 envelope topping)	1 cup	250 mL
Baked 9 inch (22 cm) pie shell, see page 140	1	1

Heat milk and pumpkin in saucepan until it boils.

Sprinkle gelatin over water in small cup. Let stand for 1 minute. Stir into pumpkin mixture. Return to a boil.

Mix next 6 ingredients in small bowl. Stir into boiling mixture. Remove from heat. Cool, then chill until a thick syrupy mixture that will mound.

Beat egg whites in small bowl until a stiff froth. Add granulated sugar gradually, beating until stiff and sugar is dissolved. Fold into chilled mixture.

Using same beaters and bowl, beat whipping cream until stiff. Fold in.

Turn into pie shell. Chill. Yield: 1 pie.

Be careful what you eat at a barbecue. Many have pits.

CHERRY PINEAPPLE PIE

Cherry and pineapple combine to make the topping for this pie.

NUTTY GRAHAM CRACKER CRUST

Butter or margarine	$^1/_3$ cup	75 mL
Graham cracker crumbs	1 cup	225 mL
Finely chopped almonds or walnuts	$^1/_4$ cup	50 mL
Brown sugar, packed	$^1/_4$ cup	50 mL

FILLING

Whipping cream (or 1 envelope topping)	1 cup	250 mL
Crushed pineapple, drained	19 oz.	540 mL
Canned cherry pie filling	19 oz.	540 mL
Cream cheese, softened	8 oz.	250 g
Granulated sugar	$^1/_3$ cup	75 mL
Vanilla	$^1/_2$ tsp.	2 mL
Almond flavoring	$^1/_4$ tsp.	1 mL
Reserved pineapple	$^1/_4$ cup	50 mL
Reserved cherry pie filling	$^1/_2$ cup	100 mL

Nutty Graham Cracker Crust: Melt butter in saucepan. Stir in graham crumbs, almonds and sugar. Press onto sides and bottom of 9 inch (22 cm) pie plate. Bake in 350°F (180°C) oven for 10 to 12 minutes. Cool.

Filling: Beat cream until stiff. Set aside.

Reserve $^1/_4$ cup (50 mL) drained pineapple and $^1/_2$ cup (125 mL) cherry pie filling to be added later to cream cheese.

In separate bowl, beat cream cheese, sugar, vanilla and almond flavoring together until smooth.

Stir in reserved pineapple and reserved pie filling. Fold in whipped cream. Turn into pie shell.

Mix remaining pineapple and cherry pie filling. Spoon over pie. Chill for at least 4 hours before serving. Yield: 1 pie.

Paré Pointer

A good memory is mostly responsible for the good old days.

A chocolate crust cradles this great filling. A super chilled pie.

CHOCOLATE COOKIE CRUST		
Butter or margarine	1/4 cup	60 mL
Chocolate cookie crumbs	1 1/3 cups	300 mL
FILLING		
Unflavored gelatin	1 x 1/4 oz.	1 x 7 g
Water	1/2 cup	125 mL
Crushed pineapple with juice	14 oz.	398 mL
Lemon juice	2 tbsp.	30 mL
Granulated sugar	1/2 cup	125 mL
Egg yolks	2	2
Egg whites, room temperature	2	2
Whipping cream (or 1 envelope topping)	1 cup	250 mL
Reserved chocolate crumbs	2 tbsp.	30 mL

Chocolate Cookie Crust: Melt butter in saucepan. Stir in wafer crumbs. Reserve 2 tbsp. (30 mL). Press rest onto bottom and sides of 9 inch (22 cm) pie plate. Bake in 350°F (180°C) oven for 10 minutes. Cool.

Filling: Sprinkle gelatin over water in small saucepan. Let stand 1 minute. Heat and stir to dissolve gelatin.

Combine pineapple with juice, lemon juice, sugar and egg yolks in saucepan over medium-low heat. Stir and bring to a boil. Remove from heat. Add gelatin mixture. Stir thoroughly. Chill until syrupy.

Beat egg whites until stiff. Fold into gelatin mixture.

Beat cream until stiff. Fold into gelatin mixture.

Pour mixture into cooled chocolate crust. Sprinkle with reserved crumbs. Chill. Yield: 1 pie.

Paré Pointer

Is a dumbwaiter someone who messes up your order?

MAPLE PECAN PIE

Small servings recommended. This is incredibly good but is quite sweet. Lighter in color than a regular pecan pie.

Sweetened condensed milk (see Note)	11 oz.	300 mL
Corn syrup	2/3 cup	150 mL
Maple flavoring	1/2 tsp.	2 mL
Salt	1/4 tsp.	1 mL
Pecans, small halves	1 cup	250 mL
Baked 9 inch (22 cm) pie shell, see page 140	1	1
WHIPPED CREAM		
Whipping cream (or 1 envelope topping)	1 cup	250 mL
Granulated sugar	2 tsp.	10 mL
Vanilla	1/2 tsp.	2 mL

Pecan halves for decorating

In medium heavy saucepan combine condensed milk, corn syrup, maple flavoring and salt. Bring to a boil stirring constantly. Boil and stir 3 minutes. Remove from heat and cool. Setting saucepan in ice water hastens cooling.

Stir in pecans. Pour into baked pie shell. Chill.

Whipped Cream: Beat cream, sugar and vanilla until stiff. Arrange on top of pie in clusters or smooth over top.

Decorate with pecans. Yield: 1 pie.

Note: A 14 oz. (398 mL) can may also be used.

Paré Pointer

If little rabbits are good, their mother gives them lollihops.

STRAWBERRY CHEESE PIE

Shining berries cover a cheese layer. Small strawberries are best for this pie. A dab of whipped cream would top it off nicely.

GLAZE

Mashed fresh strawberries	**1 cup**	**250 mL**
Granulated sugar	**³/₄ cup**	**175 mL**
Cornstarch	**3 tbsp.**	**50 mL**
Water	**¹/₂ cup**	**125 mL**

FILLING

Cream cheese, softened	**4 oz.**	**125 g**
Granulated sugar	**¹/₄ cup**	**50 mL**
Lemon juice	**1¹/₂ tsp.**	**7 mL**
Baked 9 inch (22 cm) pie shell, see page 140	**1**	**1**
Fresh strawberries	**3 cups**	**700 mL**

Glaze: Combine mashed strawberries and sugar in saucepan. Bring to a boil.

Mix cornstarch with water. Stir into boiling mixture about 1 minute until it boils and thickens. Cool.

Filling: Beat cream cheese, sugar and lemon juice together in small mixing bowl until smooth.

Spread over bottom of baked pie shell.

Arrange strawberries stem end down over cheese filling. Spoon glaze over berries. Be sure to get some on every berry. Chill 3 to 4 hours to set. Yield: 1 pie.

Paré Pointer

The maximum penalty for bigamy is two mothers-in-law.

LIGHT STRAWBERRY PIE

A perfect hot weather dessert. Garnish with a strawberry fan.

FILLING

Unflavored gelatin	1 × ¹/₄ oz.	1 × 7 g
Water	¹/₂ cup	125 mL
Granulated sugar	¹/₂ cup	125 mL
Salt	¹/₈ tsp.	0.5 mL
Lemon juice	1 tsp.	5 mL
Frozen sliced strawberries in heavy syrup, partly thawed	10 oz.	284 g
Whipping cream (or 1 envelope topping)	1 cup	250 mL
Baked 9 inch (22 cm) pie shell, see page 140	1	1

Filling: Sprinkle gelatin over water in small saucepan. Let stand 1 minute. Heat and stir to dissolve gelatin. Pour into bowl.

Add next 4 ingredients. Stir until strawberries are completely thawed. Chill until syrupy.

Beat cream in small mixing bowl until stiff. Fold into gelatin mixture.

Turn into pie shell. Chill. Yield: 1 pie.

Pictured on page 89.

CHOCOLATE MOCHA PIE

Smooth as cream and creamy good. Contains marshmallows.

FILLING

Milk	¹/₂ cup	125 mL
Large marshmallows	25	25
Semisweet chocolate chips	1 cup	250 mL
Instant coffee granules	2 tsp.	10 mL
Whipping cream (or 1 envelope topping)	1 cup	250 mL
Baked 9 inch (22 cm) pie shell, see page 140	1	1

(continued on next page)

Filling: Combine milk and marshmallows in large pot over low heat. Stir often until marshmallows melt.

Add chocolate chips and coffee granules. Stir until chips are melted. Cool.

Beat cream until stiff. Fold into cooled mixture.

Turn into pie shell. Chill for several hours. Yield: 1 pie.

CHILLED MAPLE PIE

If you have only a small container of maple syrup, save it for this recipe. Excellent flavor.

Sweetened condensed milk (see Note)	**11 oz.**	**300 mL**
Maple syrup	**³/₄ cup**	**175 mL**
Eggs	**2**	**2**
All-purpose flour	**2 tbsp.**	**30 mL**
Chopped pecans	**³/₄ cup**	**175 mL**
Baked 9 inch (22 cm) pie shell, see page 140	**1**	**1**
Whipping cream (or 1 envelope topping)	**1 cup**	**250 mL**
Granulated sugar	**1 tbsp.**	**15 mL**
Vanilla	**1 tsp.**	**5 mL**
Toasted coconut	**¹/₃ cup**	**75 mL**

Combine first 4 ingredients in saucepan. Beat until blended. Place over medium heat. Bring to a boil. Boil 5 minutes until it thickens, stirring continually. Remove from heat.

Add pecans. Stir to combine.

Pour into cooked pie shell. Chill.

Beat cream, sugar and vanilla together until stiff. Spread over pie.

Toast coconut in pan in 350°F (180°C) oven until browned. Cool. Sprinkle over whipped cream. Yield: 1 pie.

Note: A 14 oz. (398 mL) can may also be used.

PEACH ICE CREAM PIE

A peach of a pie! Also a must-try. Exquisite.

Peach flavored gelatin (jelly powder), or orange	1 × 3 oz.	1 × 85 g
Juice drained from peaches plus water if needed	1¼ cups	275 mL
Vanilla ice cream	2 cups	450 mL
Canned sliced peaches, drained, diced	2 × 14 oz.	2 × 398 mL
Baked 9 inch (22 cm) pie shell, see page 140	1	1

Whipped Cream, page 30

Combine gelatin and peach juice in saucepan over medium heat. Stir until gelatin is dissolved. Remove from heat.

Cut in ice cream. Stir until melted. Chill until syrupy if ice cream hasn't thickened it enough.

Fold in peaches. Chill until mixture will mound. Turn into pie shell. If it won't hold all filling, chill until quite firm then mound rest of filling in center. Chill.

Top with whipped cream. Yield: 1 pie.

1. Piña Colada Pie page 92
2. Key Lime Pie page 44
3. Frozen Hawaiian Pie page 82
4. Coral Reef Pie page 100

COCKTAIL PIE

With the addition of marshmallows and cream cheese, this tastes a bit like a soft fruity cheesecake.

Milk	¼ cup	60 mL
Large marshmallows	24	24
Cream cheese, softened	4 oz.	125 g
Sour cream	¾ cup	175 mL
Vanilla	1 tsp.	5 mL
Canned fruit cocktail, drained	14 oz.	398 mL
Baked Graham Cracker Crust, see page 73, reserve 2 tbsp. (30 mL) crumbs	1	1

Place milk and marshmallows in large saucepan over low heat. Stir often to hasten melting. Cool.

In small bowl beat cream cheese, sour cream and vanilla until smooth. Stir into cooled marshmallow mixture.

Fold in fruit.

Pour into pie shell. Sprinkle with reserved crumbs. Chill. Yield: 1 pie.

LEMONADE PIE

Satiny and lemony. A quick pie with few ingredients.

Baked Graham Cracker Crust, see page 73	1	1
Sweetened condensed milk (see Note)	11 oz.	300 mL
Frozen concentrated pink lemonade, thawed	6¼ oz.	178 mL
Frozen whipped topping, thawed	2 cups	500 mL

Prepare pie shell. Bake and cool.

Stir condensed milk and lemonade together. Fold in whipped topping. Pour into pie shell. Chill at least 3 hours. Yield: 1 pie.

Note: A 14 oz. (398 mL) can may also be used.

RHUBARB CHIFFON PIE

An excellent cool pie. No egg whites in this.

Thinly sliced rhubarb	2½ cups	575 mL
Water	½ cup	125 mL
Granulated sugar	1 cup	250 mL
Strawberry flavored gelatin (jelly powder)	1 × 3 oz.	1 × 85 g
Whipping cream (or 1 envelope topping)	1 cup	250 mL
Baked 9 inch (22 cm) pie shell, see page 140	1	1

Combine rhubarb, water and sugar in saucepan over medium heat. Bring to a boil stirring often. Cook until rhubarb is tender.

Stir in gelatin. Chill until syrupy.

Beat cream in small bowl until thick. Fold into thickened mixture.

Turn into pie shell. Chill. Yield: 1 pie.

ORANGE MOUSSE PIE

So smooth. So easy.

Unflavored gelatin	1 × ¼ oz.	1 × 7 g
Water	¼ cup	50 mL
Whipping cream	1 cup	250 mL
Cream cheese, cut up	8 oz.	250 g
Frozen concentrated orange juice	6 ¼ oz.	178 mL
Icing (confectioner's) sugar	¾ cup	175 mL
Vanilla	1½ tsp.	7 mL
Baked Graham Cracker Crust, see page 73	1	1

Sprinkle gelatin over water in blender. Let stand 1 minute.

Heat cream almost to boiling. Add to blender. Blend to dissolve gelatin.

Add next 4 ingredients. Blend smooth. Chill 15 to 20 minutes.

Pour into baked and cooled crust. Chill. Yield: 1 pie.

High and pretty. Serve with dabs of whipped cream if desired. Looks cool. Garnish with an orange twist.

Unflavored gelatin	1 x $^1/_4$ oz.	1 x 7 g
Granulated sugar	$^1/_2$ cup	125 mL
Salt	$^1/_8$ tsp.	0.5 mL
Water	1 cup	225 mL
Egg yolks, well beaten	3	3
Frozen concentrated orange juice, thawed	6 $^1/_4$ oz.	178 mL
Egg whites, room temperature	3	3
Granulated sugar	$^1/_4$ cup	50 mL
Baked 9 inch (22 cm) pie shell, see page 140	1	1

In heavy saucepan stir gelatin, first amount of sugar and salt together.

Add water and mix. Heat and stir until gelatin is dissolved.

Stir about $^1/_3$ cup (75 mL) gelatin mixture into egg yolks. Stir this mixture back into saucepan. Stir until it coats a metal spoon. If you draw finger across back of spoon, a path remains. Chill.

Add concentrated orange juice. Stir. Chill until mixture will mound from spoon.

Beat egg whites in bowl until a stiff froth. Beat in second amount of sugar gradually until stiff and sugar is dissolved. Fold into gelatin mixture.

Pour into pie shell. Chill. Yield: 1 pie.

Pictured on page 89.

Paré Pointer

Spies always carry insect repellant just in case their rooms are bugged.

FRESH STRAWBERRY PIE

A most attractive pie with glaze covering the whole berries. Best eaten the day it is made. Whipped cream makes a good finishing topping.

Fresh whole strawberries	3 cups	750 mL
Baked 9 inch (22 cm) pie shell, see page 140	1	1
Water	³/₄ cup	175 mL
Fresh strawberries, generous measure, mashed	1 cup	250 mL
Granulated sugar	1 cup	250 mL
Cornstarch	3 tbsp.	50 mL

Place first amount of strawberries stem end down in pie shell using just enough for 1 layer. Keep the rest until bottom ones are glazed.

Combine water and mashed strawberries in saucepan over medium heat. Bring to a boil. Simmer about 5 minutes. Strain. Return liquid to saucepan.

Mix sugar and cornstarch in small bowl. Add to juice. Heat and stir until it boils and thickens. Cool to lukewarm. Spoon some over berries in pie shell. Place remaining berries over top and spoon rest of glaze over them. A simple method is to toss berries in glaze and turn into pie shell. Large berries may be cut. More berries may be used if desired. Chill at least 2 hours. Yield: 1 pie.

GRAPEFRUIT CHIFFON PIE

A delicious citrus pie. Tastes so grapefruity. Very light in texture.

Unflavored gelatin	1 x ¹/₄ oz.	1 x 7 g
Grapefruit juice	¹/₄ cup	60 mL
Grated grapefruit rind (optional)	¹/₂ tsp.	2 mL
Grapefruit juice	1³/₄ cups	400 mL
Granulated sugar	¹/₃ cup	75 mL
Whipping cream (or 1 envelope topping)	1 cup	250 mL
Baked Graham Cracker Crust, see page 73	1	1

(continued on next page)

Sprinkle gelatin over first amount of grapefruit juice in small saucepan. Let stand 1 minute. Heat and stir to dissolve. Remove from heat.

Add rind, second amount of grapefruit juice and sugar. Stir to dissolve sugar. Chill until syrupy.

Beat cream until stiff. Fold into thickening mixture.

Pour into pie crust. Chill. Decorate with thin slices of pink grapefruit if desired. Yield: 1 pie.

MILLIONAIRE PIE

Cool is the word for this yummy pie.

FILLING

Butter or margarine, softened	6 tbsp.	100 mL
Icing (confectioner's) sugar	1½ cups	350 mL
Egg	1	1
Vanilla	¼ tsp.	1 mL
Salt	⅛ tsp.	0.5 mL
Baked 9 inch (22 cm) pie shell, see page 140	1	1
Whipping cream (or 1 envelope topping)	1 cup	250 mL
Crushed pineapple, drained	19 oz.	540 mL
Finely chopped pecans or walnuts (optional)	⅓ cup	75 mL

Whipped Cream, see page 30
Ground pecans, sprinkle

Filling: Measure first 5 ingredients into mixing bowl. Beat until smooth.

Spread in bottom of pie shell. Chill.

Beat whipping cream until stiff.

Fold in pineapple and chopped pecans. Spread over filling. Chill.

Garnish with whipped cream. Sprinkle with ground pecans. Yield: 1 pie.

Pictured on page 125.

GRASSHOPPER PIE

A creamy minty smoothy. Very showy in a chocolate crumb crust. Also known as Crème de Menthe pie.

CHOCOLATE COOKIE CRUST		
Butter or margarine	¹/₃ cup	75 mL
Chocolate wafer crumbs	1¹/₄ cups	275 mL

FILLING		
Milk	¹/₂ cup	125 mL
Large marshmallows	24	24
Crème de menthe, green	¹/₄ cup	60 mL
Crème de cacao, clear	2 tbsp.	30 mL
Whipping cream (or 1 envelope topping)	1 cup	250 mL

Chocolate Cookie Crust: Melt butter in saucepan. Stir in chocolate crumbs. Reserve 2 tbsp. (30 mL). Press remaining crumbs onto bottom and sides of 9 inch (22 cm) pie plate. Chill.

Filling: Heat milk in large heavy saucepan. Add marshmallows and stir until melted. Cool.

Stir in crème de menthe and crème de cacao.

Beat cream in small bowl until stiff. Fold into marshmallow mixture. Turn into pie shell. Sprinkle with reserved crumbs. Chill. Yield: 1 pie.

Note: If you prefer, you may omit liqueurs and add a few drops of peppermint flavoring to taste, along with a bit of green food coloring. Add extra milk in place of liqueur.

Pictured on page 89.

PINK VELVET PIE

A slightly tart yet mellow lemon flavor. Satiny smooth in texture.

Chilled Chocolate Graham Cracker Crust, see page 85	1	1
Cream cheese, softened	8 oz.	250 g
Sweetened condensed milk (see Note)	11 oz.	300 mL
Frozen concentrated pink lemonade, thawed	6 ¹/₄ oz.	178 mL
Frozen whipped topping, thawed	2 cups	500 mL

(continued on next page)

Prepare crust in 9 inch (22 cm) pie plate. Chill rather than bake.

Beat cream cheese and condensed milk until smooth. Add concentrated lemonade. Beat in.

Fold in whipped topping. Pour into pie shell. Chill 2 hours before cutting. Pie may also be frozen. Yield: 1 pie.

Note: A 14 oz. (398 mL) can may also be used.

CHEESE PIE

This crowning glory is inches deep. Contains pineapple and cream cheese with red cherries for color. A show off pie.

Cream cheese, softened	8 oz.	250 mL
Granulated sugar	$2/3$ cup	150 mL
Crushed pineapple, drained	19 oz.	540 mL
Whipping cream (or 1 envelope topping)	1 cup	250 mL
Baked Graham Cracker Crust, see page 73	1	1
WHIPPED CREAM		
Whipping cream (or 1 envelope topping)	1 cup	250 mL
Granulated sugar	2 tsp.	10 mL
Vanilla	$1/2$ tsp.	2 mL
Medium coconut	$1/2$ cup	125 mL
Maraschino cherries, chopped	8	8

Beat cream cheese and sugar in mixing bowl until smooth.

Add pineapple and stir.

Beat cream until stiff. Fold in.

Turn into pie shell. Chill.

Whipped Cream: Beat cream, sugar and vanilla in small mixing bowl until stiff.

Fold in coconut and cherries. Spread over pie. Chill. Yield: 1 pie.

KEY LIME PIE

This looks so cool it makes you feel cooler on a hot day. Garnish with lime slices.

Egg yolks	3	3
Sweetened condensed milk (see Note)	11 oz.	300 mL
Lime juice	1/2 cup	125 mL
Drops of green food color (optional)	2-4	2-4
Baked 9 inch (22 cm) pie shell, see page 140	1	1
MERINGUE		
Egg whites, room temperature	3	3
Cream of tartar	1/4 tsp.	1 mL
Granulated sugar	6 tbsp.	100 mL

Beat egg yolks until smooth. Add condensed milk, lime juice and green food color, if using. Beat.

Pour into pie shell.

Meringue: Beat egg whites and cream of tartar in small mixing bowl until a stiff froth. Gradually add sugar, beating until stiff and sugar is dissolved. Spread over filling sealing to crust all around. Bake in 350°F (180°C) oven about 10 to 15 minutes until browned. Cool for about 1 hour then chill at least 3 hours. Yield: 1 pie.

Note: A 14 oz. (398 mL) can may also be used.

Pictured on page 35.

CREAMY LIME PIE: Omit eggs. Beat 1 cup (250 mL) whipping cream until stiff. Fold into filling. Chill. Serve with additional whipped cream on each piece.

CHILLED CHERRY PIE

A pretty white pie smothered with red cherry pie filling.

Sweetened condensed milk (see Note)	11 oz.	300 mL
Cream cheese, softened	8 oz.	250 g
Lemon juice	1/3 cup	75 mL
Vanilla	1 tsp.	5 mL
Baked Graham Cracker Crust, see page 73	1	1
Canned cherry pie filling	19 oz.	540 mL

(continued on next page)

Beat condensed milk and cream cheese together until smooth. Add lemon juice, and vanilla. Mix.

Pour into pie shell. Chill about 3 hours until set.

Spread cherry pie filling over top. Use all of can or just part. Chill. Yield: 1 pie.

Note: A 14 oz. (398 mL) can may also be used.

Pictured on page 107.

PINEAPPLE CHIFFON PIE

Just a real good pineapple flavored frothy pie. Made from pineapple juice.

Pineapple juice	**1¹/₂ cups**	**350 mL**
Unflavored gelatin	**1 x ¹/₄ oz.**	**1 x 7 g**
Granulated sugar	**³/₄ cup**	**175 mL**
Lemon juice	**1 tbsp.**	**15 mL**
Salt	**¹/₂ tsp.**	**2 mL**
Egg yolks, beaten	**2**	**2**
Egg whites, room temperature	**2**	**2**
Whipping cream (or 1 envelope topping)	**1 cup**	**250 mL**
Baked 9 inch (22 cm) pie shell, see page 140	**1**	**1**

Pour pineapple juice into saucepan. Sprinkle gelatin over top. Let stand for 1 minute. Heat and stir to dissolve.

Add sugar, lemon juice and salt. Stir. Bring to a boil.

Mix about ¹/₂ cup (125 mL) gelatin mixture into egg yolks. Pour into saucepan stirring until it returns to a boil. Cool then chill until quite syrupy. Stir now and then while chilling.

Beat egg whites until stiff. Fold into thickened mixture.

Using same bowl and beaters, beat cream until stiff. Fold in.

Fold into pie shell. Chill. Yield: 1 pie.

CHOCOLATE MINT PIE

A terrific combination. Just the right amount of mint.

FILLING

Butter or margarine, softened	**³/₄ cup**	**175 mL**
Icing (confectioner's) sugar	**1¹/₂ cups**	**375 mL**
Unsweetened baking chocolate squares, melted and cooled	**3 × 1 oz.**	**3 × 28 g**
Eggs	**3**	**3**
Peppermint flavoring	**¹/₂ tsp.**	**2 mL**
Baked Nutty Graham Cracker Crust, see page 28	**1**	**1**

Whipped Cream, see page 30
Mint leaves for garnish

Filling: Cream butter and icing sugar. Add melted chocolate. Beat well.

Beat in eggs 1 at a time. Add peppermint flavoring. Mix.

Pour into pie crust. Chill. May be frozen at this point. Thaw to use.

To serve, garnish with whipped cream and mint leaves. Yield: 1 pie.

LEMON CHIFFON PIE

A pretty pie. Delicate in texture and flavor.

Unflavored gelatin	**1 × ¹/₄ oz.**	**1 × 7 g**
Lemon juice	**¹/₄ cup**	**60 mL**
Water	**1 cup**	**250 mL**
Granulated sugar	**²/₃ cup**	**150 mL**
Grated rind of lemon	**1**	**1**
Egg whites, room temperature	**3**	**3**
Baked Graham Cracker Crust, see page 73, reserve 2 tbsp. (30 mL) crumbs	**1**	**1**

Whipped Cream, see page 30 (optional)

(continued on next page)

Sprinkle gelatin over lemon juice in small saucepan. Let stand for 1 minute. Heat and stir to dissolve gelatin.

Combine water, sugar and lemon rind in saucepan. Bring to a boil stirring often. Stir in gelatin mixture until it dissolves. Chill until it will mound from spoon.

Beat egg whites until stiff. Fold into thickened mixture.

Turn into pie crust. Sprinkle with reserved crumbs. Chill.

Serve topped with whipped cream. Yield: 1 pie.

CHERRY PINE PIE

The perky flavor comes from the raspberry gelatin. Walnuts add a touch of crunch. Makes two pies.

Crushed pineapple with juice	19 oz.	540 mL
Cornstarch	1 tbsp.	15 mL
Raspberry flavored gelatin (jelly powder)	1 × 3 oz.	1 × 85 g
Canned cherry pie filling	19 oz.	540 mL
Granulated sugar	3/4 cup	175 mL
Almond flavoring	1/4 tsp.	1 mL
Chopped walnuts	3/4 cup	175 mL
Baked Graham Cracker Crusts, see page 73	2	2
WHIPPED CREAM		
Whipping cream (or 2 envelopes topping)	2 cups	500 mL
Granulated sugar	4 tsp.	20 mL
Vanilla	1 tsp.	5 mL

Combine pineapple with juice, cornstarch and raspberry gelatin in saucepan. Heat and stir until it boils and thickens. Remove from heat.

Add pie filling, sugar, almond flavoring and walnuts. Stir.

Pour into pie shells. Chill.

Whipped Cream: Beat cream, sugar, and vanilla until stiff. Spoon onto each pie. Yield: 2 pies.

FRENCH SILK PIE

A rich pie with a smooth, silky texture.

Butter or margarine, softened	½ cup	125 mL
Granulated sugar	¾ cup	175 mL
Vanilla	1 tsp.	5 mL
Semisweet baking chocolate squares, melted	2 × 1 oz.	2 × 28 g
Cocoa	1 tbsp.	15 mL
Eggs	2	2
Baked Graham Cracker Crust, see page 73	1	1
WHIPPED CREAM		
Whipping cream	1 cup	250 mL
Granulated sugar	2 tsp.	10 mL
Vanilla	½ tsp.	2 mL
Chocolate curls or toasted slivered almonds for garnish		

Cream butter, sugar and vanilla well.

Add melted chocolate and cocoa. Mix.

Beat in eggs 1 at a time beating 5 minutes at medium speed after each addition.

Pour into pie shell. Chill at least 4 hours.

Whipped Cream: Beat cream, sugar and vanilla together in small mixing bowl until stiff. Spread over pie.

Garnish with chocolate curls or toasted slivered almonds. Yield: 1 pie.

Pictured on page 71.

A mother bee was overheard talking to her bad baby bee, "Just beehive yourself".

A refreshing pie that's different.

Watermelon	1/4 - 1/2	1/4 - 1/2
Unflavored gelatin powder	2 x 1/4 oz.	2 x 7 g
Watermelon juice	1 cup	250 mL
Granulated sugar	3/4 cup	175 mL
Lemon juice	1 tbsp.	15 mL
Watermelon juice	1 1/2 cups	350 mL
Egg whites, room temperature	2	2
Whipping cream (or 1 envelope topping)	1 cup	250 mL
Baked Graham Cracker Crust, see page 73, make 10 inch (25 cm) crust	1	1
Watermelon balls for garnish		

Cut about 1/4 of medium watermelon into small cubes. Press through food mill to remove seeds and to get 2 1/2 cups (600 mL) of pulpy juice.

Sprinkle gelatin over first amount of watermelon juice in small saucepan. Let stand 1 minute. Heat and stir to dissolve. Remove from heat.

Stir in sugar. Add lemon juice and second amount of watermelon juice. Chill until syrupy.

Beat egg whites until stiff. Fold into gelatin mixture.

Beat whipping cream until stiff. Fold into gelatin mixture.

Turn into pie shell. Use melon baller to scoop out balls from remaining watermelon. Chill balls and pie separately about 4 hours. Just before serving arrange melon balls on top. Yield: 1 pie.

Paré Pointer

All their lady sheep wear ewe-niforms.

CHILLED FRUIT COCKTAIL PIE

A lemony, good, full pie. Adding banana to the fruit greatly enhances the taste of this pie.

Sweetened condensed milk, (see Note)	11 oz.	300 mL
Lemon juice	1/2 cup	125 mL
Banana, peeled and cubed	1	1
Canned fruit cocktail, drained	14 oz.	398 mL
Whipping cream (or 1 envelope topping)	1 cup	250 mL
Baked Graham Cracker Crust, see page 73, reserve 2 tbsp., (30 mL) crumbs	1	1

Stir condensed milk and lemon juice together in bowl.

Fold in banana and fruit cocktail.

Beat cream in small bowl until stiff. Fold into fruit mixture.

Turn into pie crust. Sprinkle with reserved crumbs. Chill. Yield: 1 pie.

Note: A 14 oz. (398 mL) can may also be used.

GLAZED BLUEBERRY PIE

A blueberry topping covers a cream cheese base. A lovely chilled pie.

Cream cheese, softened	8 oz.	250 g
Granulated sugar	1/2 cup	125 mL
Lemon juice	1 tbsp.	15 mL
Baked 9 inch (22 cm) pie shell, see page 140	1	1
Blueberries, fresh or frozen	2 cups	450 mL
Granulated sugar	3/4 cup	175 mL
Cornstarch	3 tbsp.	50 mL
Water	1/2 cup	125 mL
Blueberries, fresh or frozen	1 cup	225 mL
Lemon juice	1 tbsp.	15 mL

(continued on next page)

Beat cream cheese, first amounts of sugar and lemon juice in small mixing bowl until smooth.

Spread in bottom of pie shell. Chill.

Pour first amount of blueberries over cheese mixture.

Combine remaining 5 ingredients in saucepan. Heat and stir until it boils and thickens. Cool. Spoon evenly over blueberries in pie shell. You may not need to use quite all of it. Chill. Yield: 1 pie.

GELATIN CHERRY PIE

Stunning! A pink layer topped with red cherries and whipped cream.

GRAHAM NUT CRUST		
Butter or margarine	1/3 cup	75 mL
Graham cracker crumbs	1 cup	225 mL
Ground almonds	1/4 cup	60 mL
Granulated sugar	3 tbsp.	50 mL
FILLING		
Cherry flavored gelatin (jelly powder)	1 × 3 oz.	1 × 85 g
Boiling water	1 cup	225 mL
Canned cherry pie filling	1/2 × 19 oz.	1/2 × 540 mL
Whipping cream (or 1 1/2 envelopes topping)	1 1/2 cups	375 mL
Reserved whipped cream	1 cup	250 mL
Canned cherry pie filling	1/2 × 19 oz.	1/2 × 540 mL

Graham Nut Crust: Melt butter in saucepan. Stir in graham crumbs, almonds and sugar. Press on bottom and sides of 9 inch (22 cm) pie plate. Bake in 350°F (180°C) oven for 10 to 12 minutes. Cool.

Filling: Stir cherry gelatin into boiling water in bowl until dissolved.

Stir in 1/2 can cherry pie filling. Chill until syrupy.

Beat cream until stiff. Reserve 1 cup (250 mL). Fold the remaining cream into thickened mixture. Turn into pie shell.

Pipe reserved cream around outside edge. Spoon second half of pie filling around edge inside of cream. Chill. Yield: 1 pie.

CREAMY LEMON PIE

This is no trouble to make and is lovely the next day.

Sweetened condensed milk (see Note)	11 oz.	300 mL
Grated rind of lemon	1	1
Lemon juice	1/2 cup	125 mL
Egg yolks	2	2
Baked 9 inch (22 cm) pie shell, see page 140	1	1
MERINGUE		
Egg whites, room temperature	2	2
Cream of tartar	1/4 tsp.	1 mL
Granulated sugar	1/4 cup	60 mL

Combine first 4 ingredients in small mixing bowl. Beat together well.

Pour into pie shell.

Meringue: Beat egg whites and cream of tartar in clean small mixing bowl until a stiff froth. Add sugar gradually, beating until stiff and sugar is dissolved. Spoon over filling sealing well to outer edge all around. Brown in 350°F (180°C) oven about 10 minutes. Cool. Chill thoroughly before serving. Yield: 1 pie.

Note: A 14 oz. (398 mL) can may also be used.

1. Upside Down Apple Pie page 119
2. Mock Apple Pie page 134
3. Crustless Apple Pie page 57
4. Dutch Apple Pie page 93

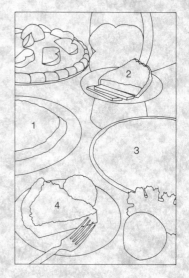

This has the flavor of regular sour cream pie but does not require baking. Frothy light.

Unflavored gelatin (1/2 envelope)	1 1/2 tsp.	7 mL
Water	1/4 cup	50 mL
Coarsely chopped raisins	1/2 cup	125 mL
Brown sugar, packed	3/4 cup	175 mL
Cinnamon	1/2 tsp.	2 mL
Nutmeg	1/8 tsp.	0.5 mL
Egg yolks, beaten	2	2
Sour cream	1/2 cup	125 mL
Egg whites, room temperature	2	2
Whipping cream (or 1 envelope topping)	1 cup	250 mL
Baked 9 inch (22 cm) pie shell, see page 140	1	1

Sprinkle gelatin over water in small saucepan. Let stand 1 minute. Heat and stir to dissolve gelatin.

Add raisins and cool. Turn into medium bowl.

Stir in next 5 ingredients. Chill until it mounds.

Beat egg whites in small mixing bowl until stiff. Fold into mixture.

Using same bowl and beaters, beat cream until stiff. Fold into mixture.

Turn into pie shell. Chill. Yield: 1 pie.

He can marry anyone he pleases. The trouble is he hasn't pleased anyone yet.

SWEET PINEAPPLE PIE

Good height to this pie. The flavors of coconut, pineapple and nuts all come through. Very quick and easy.

Sweetened condensed milk (see Note)	11 oz.	300 mL
Lemon juice	3 tbsp.	50 mL
Coconut, medium or flake	³/₄ cup	175 mL
Chopped pecans or walnuts	³/₄ cup	175 mL
Crushed pineapple, drained	14 oz.	398 mL
Frozen whipped topping, thawed	2 cups	500 mL
Baked Graham Cracker Crust, see page 73	1	1

Mix first 5 ingredients in bowl in order given.

Fold in whipped topping.

Turn into pie shell. Chill. Yield: 1 pie.

Note: A 14 oz. (398 mL) can may also be used.

IMPOSSIBLE PIE

Makes its own crust. Serve with a blueberry or lemon sauce.

Coconut, medium or flake	1 cup	250 mL
Milk	2 cups	450 mL
Eggs	4	4
Butter or margarine	¹/₄ cup	50 mL
Tea biscuit mix	¹/₂ cup	125 mL
Granulated sugar	1 cup	225 mL
Vanilla	1¹/₂ tsp.	7 mL

Sprinkle coconut into bottom of greased 9 inch (22 cm) pie plate.

Combine remaining 6 ingredients in blender. Blend smooth. Pour over coconut. Bake on bottom shelf in 350° F (180° C) oven for about 45 to 55 minutes until an inserted knife comes out clean. Yield: 1 pie.

CRUSTLESS APPLE PIE

You can still enjoy a creamy apple pie even if you don't want any pastry.

Cooking apples, peeled, cored and cut up (McIntosh is good)	5 cups	1.13 L
Granulated sugar	1 cup	250 mL
Cinnamon	1 tsp.	5 mL
Biscuit mix	1/2 cup	125 mL
Eggs	2	2
Milk	3/4 cup	175 mL
Butter or margarine, softened	2 tbsp.	30 mL
Vanilla	1 tsp.	5 mL
TOPPING		
All-purpose flour	2/3 cup	150 mL
Brown sugar, packed	1/3 cup	75 mL
Salt	1/4 tsp.	1 mL
Butter or margarine	3 tbsp.	50 mL

Place apples in greased 10 inch (25 cm) pie plate. Pour sugar over top. Sprinkle cinnamon over sugar.

Measure next 5 ingredients into blender. Blend smooth. This may also be beaten in bowl until smooth. Pour over pie.

Topping: Mix flour, sugar, salt and butter until crumbly. Scatter over apples. Bake in 350°F (180°C) oven about 50 minutes until apples are cooked. Yield: 1 pie.

Pictured on page 53.

As hunters drove by in a jeep, one lion was heard to say "Look, meals on wheels!"

CHERRY NO-CRUST PIE

You will never even miss the pastry.

Milk	1 cup	250 mL
Eggs	2	2
Biscuit mix	1/2 cup	125 mL
Granulated sugar	1/4 cup	50 mL
Almond flavoring	1/4 tsp.	1 mL
Canned cherry pie filling	19 oz.	540 mL
TOPPING		
All-purpose flour	3/4 cup	175 mL
Brown sugar, packed	1/2 cup	125 mL
Cinnamon	1/4 tsp.	1 mL
Salt	1/4 tsp.	1 mL
Butter or margarine	1/4 cup	50 mL

Place milk, eggs, biscuit mix and sugar in blender. Blend about 15 seconds until smooth. Pour into greased 10 inch (25 cm) pie plate.

Stir almond flavoring into cherry pie filling. Spoon dabs here and there evenly over mixture in pie plate. Bake on bottom shelf in 400°F (200°C) oven for about 35 minutes.

Topping: Mix all 5 ingredients until crumbly. Sprinkle over partially baked pie. Return to oven and bake about 10 minutes until browned. Serve chilled. Yield: 1 pie.

NO-CRUST FUDGE PIE

A moist fudgy center satisfies a longing for a chocolate dessert. Freezes well.

Eggs	3	3
Granulated sugar	1 1/4 cups	275 mL
All-purpose flour	1/4 cup	50 mL
Vanilla	1 tsp.	5 mL
Unsweetened baking chocolate squares, cut up	3 × 1 oz.	3 × 28 g
Butter or margarine	1/2 cup	125 mL
Vanilla ice cream or Whipped Cream, see page 30		

(continued on next page)

Beat eggs in mixing bowl until smooth. Add sugar, flour and vanilla. Beat to mix.

Melt chocolate squares and butter in small saucepan over low heat. Add to egg mixture and beat until mixed. Pour into greased 9 inch (22 cm) pie plate. Bake in 350°F (180°C) oven for about 35 minutes. Center will be a bit soft and moist when tested with toothpick.

Serve warm with ice cream or whipped cream. Yield: 1 pie.

IMPOSSIBLE PUMPKIN PIE

Very quick to make. No crust required.

Evaporated milk	13$^1/_2$ oz.	385 mL
Canned pumpkin, without spices	14 oz.	398 mL
Granulated sugar	$^3/_4$ cup	175 mL
Biscuit mix	$^1/_2$ cup	125 mL
Eggs	2	2
Vanilla	1 tsp.	5 mL
Cinnamon	1 tsp.	5 mL
Ginger	$^1/_2$ tsp.	2 mL
Cloves	$^1/_4$ tsp.	1 mL

Whipped Cream, see page 30

Combine first 9 ingredients in blender. Blend until smooth. Pour into greased 9 inch (22 cm) pie plate. Bake in 350°F (180°C) oven about 50 to 55 minutes until an inserted knife comes out clean. Cool.

Spread whipped cream over top before serving. Yield: 1 pie.

Paré Pointer

She thought he was one in a million, but actually he was won in a raffle.

CHOCOLATE COCONUT PIE

Good chocolate flavor. Good coconut flavor too.

Semisweet baking chocolate squares, cut up	4 × 1 oz.	4 × 28 g
Butter or margarine	1/4 cup	50 mL
Evaporated milk	13 1/2 oz.	385 mL
Eggs, lightly beaten	3	3
Granulated sugar	1/2 cup	125 mL
Flake coconut	1 1/3 cups	300 mL
Unbaked 9 inch (22 cm) pie shell, see page 140	1	1
Whipped Cream, see page 30		

Combine chocolate, butter and evaporated milk in medium saucepan over low heat. Stir often until chocolate is melted. Remove from heat.

Mix in eggs, sugar and coconut.

Turn into pie shell. Bake in 400°F (200°C) oven about 30 minutes until set. Cool.

Serve with whipped cream. Yield: 1 pie.

COTTAGE CHEESE PIE

A different way to use cottage cheese. Contains raisins for added interest.

Eggs	2	2
Dry cottage cheese, mashed fine	2 cups	500 mL
All-purpose flour	2 tbsp.	30 mL
Granulated sugar	1 cup	250 mL
Salt	1/4 tsp.	1 mL
Vanilla	1 tsp.	5 mL
Milk	1 cup	250 mL
Raisins	1 cup	250 mL
Unbaked 9 inch (22 cm) pie shell, see page 140	1	1
Cinnamon	1/4 tsp.	1 mL

(continued on next page)

Beat eggs in mixing bowl until smooth. Add next 5 ingredients. Beat until blended.

Stir in milk and raisins.

Pour into pie shell. Bake on bottom shelf in 325°F (160°C) oven about 45 to 60 minutes until an inserted knife comes out clean.

Sprinkle with cinnamon upon removal from oven. Yield: 1 pie.

BUTTERSCOTCH PIE

Real old fashioned goodness.

Milk	2 cups	450 mL
Dark brown sugar, packed (not Demerara)	1¼ cups	275 mL
All-purpose flour	6 tbsp.	100 mL
Salt	¼ tsp.	1 mL
Vanilla	1 tsp.	5 mL
Egg yolks	3	3
Milk	¼ cup	50 mL
Baked 9 inch (22 cm) pie shell, see page 140	1	1
MERINGUE		
Egg whites, room temperature	3	3
Vinegar	½ tsp.	2 mL
Granulated sugar	6 tbsp.	100 mL

Heat milk in heavy saucepan until it boils.

Meanwhile mix sugar and flour in bowl. Mix in salt, vanilla, egg yolks and milk. Stir into boiling milk until it boils and thickens.

Pour into pie shell.

Meringue: Beat egg whites and vinegar in bowl until a firm froth. Add sugar gradually, beating until stiff and sugar is dissolved. Spread over pie pushing to seal well to edge all around. Bake in 350°F (180°C) oven about 10 minutes until golden. Chill several hours. Yield: 1 pie.

Pictured on page 143.

SOUR CREAM PIE

This family favorite is old, old. Nobody can tell what kind it is. Ground raisins make all the difference.

Sour cream	1 cup	250 mL
Egg	1	1
Granulated sugar	1/2 cup	125 mL
Cinnamon	1/4 tsp.	1 mL
Nutmeg	1/4 tsp.	1 mL
Allspice	1/4 tsp.	1 mL
Salt	1/8 tsp.	0.5 mL
Baking soda, just a pinch		
Raisins, ground	1 cup	250 mL
Unbaked 9 inch (22 cm) pie shell, see page 140	1	1

Combine first 8 ingredients in bowl. Mix well.

Add raisins. They will mix better after 30 minutes or so as they soften. If you have a food processor combine all ingredients except pie shell and process until raisins are ground.

Pour into pie shell. Bake on bottom shelf in 350°F (180°C) oven about 35 to 40 minutes until set. Yield: 1 pie.

SOUR CREAM TARTS: Bake in tart shells. Especially good.

Pictured on page 125.

CUSTARD PIE

A pudding in a pie.

Milk	2 1/3 cups	525 mL
Eggs	4	4
Granulated sugar	1/2 cup	125 mL
Salt	1/4 tsp.	1 mL
Vanilla	1 tsp.	5 mL
Unbaked 9 inch (22 cm) pie shell, see page 140	1	1
Nutmeg	1/4 tsp.	1 mL

(continued on next page)

Heat milk in heavy saucepan until scalded.

Meanwhile in small bowl stir eggs briskly with a spoon. Mix in sugar, salt and vanilla. Slowly stir into hot milk.

Grease inside of pie shell with softened margarine or lightly beaten egg white. Pour filling into pie shell. Sprinkle with nutmeg. Bake on bottom shelf in 450°F (230°C) oven for 10 minutes. Lower heat to 325°F (160°C) and bake for about 30 minutes until an inserted knife comes out clean. Cool. Yield: 1 pie.

CARAMEL PIE

You may choose to serve this with whipped cream rather than meringue. Good flavor.

Brown sugar, packed	1¼ cups	275 mL
Butter or margarine	2 tbsp.	30 mL
Water	2 tbsp.	30 mL
Water	1 cup	225 mL
Egg yolks	3	3
Milk	¾ cup	175 mL
Cornstarch	2 tbsp.	30 mL
Baked 9 inch (22 cm) pie shell, see page 140	1	1
MERINGUE		
Egg whites, room temperature	3	3
Cream of tartar	¼ tsp.	1 mL
Granulated sugar	⅓ cup	75 mL

Combine sugar, butter and first amount of water in heavy saucepan. Heat and stir until it boils. Stir often to prevent burning while it continues to boil, about 5 minutes. It turns a coppery brown and thickens.

Add second amount of water. Stir and return to a boil.

Mix egg yolks, milk and cornstarch in small bowl. Stir into boiling mixture until it boils and thickens.

Pour into pie shell.

Meringue: Beat egg whites and cream of tartar until a stiff froth. Beat in sugar gradually, until stiff and sugar is dissolved. Spread over pie, sealing well to edge all around. Bake in 375°F (190°C) oven about 10 minutes until golden. Yield: 1 pie.

BLACK BOTTOM PIE

There is a chocolate layer on the pie crust, covered with a tender layer of chilled custard which has a hint of rum. For an extra touch, drizzle with melted chocolate.

CUSTARD

Milk	2 cups	450 mL
Granulated sugar	1/2 cup	125 mL
Cornstarch	2 tbsp.	30 mL
Egg yolks	3	3
Vanilla	1 tsp.	5 mL
Salt	1/2 tsp.	2 mL

CHOCOLATE LAYER

Reserved custard	1 cup	250 mL
Semisweet chocolate chips	1/2 cup	125 mL
Baked 9 inch (22 cm) pie shell, see page 140	1	1

LIGHT LAYER

Unflavored gelatin	1 x 1/4 oz.	1 x 7 g
Water	1/4 cup	50 mL
Remaining custard		
Rum flavoring	2 tsp.	10 mL
Egg whites, room temperature	3	3
Cream of tartar	1/4 tsp.	1 mL
Granulated sugar	1/2 cup	125 mL

Custard: Bring milk to a boil in saucepan over medium heat.

Meanwhile mix sugar, cornstarch, egg yolks, vanilla and salt in a small bowl. Stir into boiling milk until it returns to a boil. Remove from heat.

Chocolate Layer: Pour 1 cup (250 mL) hot custard into small bowl. Add chocolate chips. Stir until chips are melted.

Pour into pie shell. Chill.

Light layer: Sprinkle gelatin over water. Let stand 1 minute. Add to remaining hot custard. Stir to dissolve gelatin. Add rum flavoring. Chill until syrupy. Mixture should mound slightly when dropped from spoon.

Beat egg whites and cream of tartar until a stiff froth. Add sugar gradually, beating until stiff. Fold into thickened custard. Pour over chocolate layer. Chill. Yield: 1 pie.

Pictured on page 17.

LEMON MERINGUE PIE

This from-scratch pie is best made and eaten the same day. Lemony and light.

FILLING

Granulated sugar	1 cup	250 mL
Cornstarch	3 tbsp.	50 mL
Hot water	2 cups	500 mL
Egg yolks	3	3
Juice of lemons	2	2
Butter or margarine	1 tbsp.	15 mL
Salt	$1/4$ tsp.	1 mL
Baked 9 inch (22 cm) pie shell, see page 140	1	1

MERINGUE

Egg whites, room temperature	3	3
Cream of tartar	$1/4$ tsp.	1 mL
Granulated sugar	6 tbsp.	100 mL

Filling: Put sugar and cornstarch in medium saucepan. Stir to mix. Stir in water and egg yolks. Stir over medium heat until it boils. Boil about 1 minute. Remove from heat.

Stir in lemon juice, butter and salt. Cool.

Spoon filling into pie shell.

Meringue: Beat egg whites and cream of tartar until a stiff froth. Add sugar gradually while beating until stiff and sugar is dissolved. You should feel no graininess when rubbing a bit of meringue between fingers. Pile onto filling being sure to seal well to pastry all around. Bake near top of 350°F (180°C) oven about 10 to 15 minutes until browned. Yield: 1 pie.

LIME MERINGUE PIE: Use lime juice instead of lemon. Add about 2 tsp. (10 mL) finely grated lime rind if desired.

BLACK BOTTOM LEMON PIE: Sprinkle 1 cup (250 mL) semisweet chocolate chips in baked pie shell. Heat in 350°F (180°C) oven until melted. Spread over bottom. Chill. Proceed to make lemon filling as recipe states.

PEANUT BUTTER CREAM PIE

A light peanut flavor and a cream filling.

FILLING

Milk	**2¹/₄ cups**	**500 mL**
Granulated sugar	**²/₃ cup**	**150 mL**
Cornstarch	**3 tbsp.**	**50 mL**
Egg yolks	**3**	**3**
Milk	**¹/₄ cup**	**60 mL**
Vanilla	**1 tsp.**	**5 mL**

CRUMBLES

Smooth peanut butter	**¹/₂ cup**	**125 mL**
Icing (confectioner's) sugar	**1 cup**	**250 mL**
Baked 9 inch (22 cm) pie shell, see page 140	**1**	**1**

MERINGUE

Egg whites, room temperature	**3**	**3**
Cream of tartar	**¹/₄ tsp.**	**1 mL**
Granulated sugar	**6 tbsp.**	**100 mL**

Filling: Heat milk in heavy saucepan until it boils.

Meanwhile stir sugar and cornstarch together in small bowl. Mix in egg yolks, milk and vanilla. Stir into boiling milk until it boils and thickens. Remove from heat. Cool for 30 minutes.

Crumbles: Mix peanut butter and icing sugar until mealy.

Sprinkle about ²/₃ crumbles over bottom of pie shell. Pour filling over top. Sprinkle with remaining crumbles.

Meringue: Beat egg whites and cream of tartar until a stiff froth. Gradually beat in sugar until stiff and sugar is dissolved. Spread over filling sealing well to edge of pie shell. Bake in 350°F (180°C) oven about 10 to 15 minutes until browned. Yield: 1 pie.

Note: Meringue may be omitted and Whipped Cream, page 30, spread over chilled pie.

Paré Pointer

Try a ghoul's breakfast - dreaded wheat.

Good flavor to this chilled pie.

Milk	2¼ cups	500 mL
Granulated sugar	⅔ cup	150 mL
All-purpose flour	½ cup	125 mL
Salt	¼ tsp.	1 mL
FILLING		
Egg yolks	3	3
Butter or margarine	2 tbsp.	30 mL
Vanilla	1 tsp.	5 mL
Coconut, flaked or thread	1 cup	250 mL
Baked 9 inch (22 cm) pie shell, see page 140	1	1
WHIPPED CREAM		
Whipping cream (or 1 envelope topping)	1 cup	250 mL
Granulated sugar	1 tbsp.	15 mL
Vanilla	¾ tsp.	4 mL
Toasted thread coconut	⅓ cup	75 mL

Bring milk to a boil in heavy saucepan.

Mix sugar, flour and salt well in small bowl. Stir into boiling milk until it boils and thickens.

Filling: Place egg yolks, butter and vanilla in small bowl. Add about ½ cup (125 mL) hot mixture. Stir. Pour egg mixture into hot mixture all at once while stirring continuously until it boils and thickens.

Add coconut. Stir. Cool 15 minutes.

Pour into pie shell. Place plastic wrap directly on surface of filling. Chill several hours.

Whipped Cream: Beat cream, sugar and vanilla in small mixing bowl until stiff. Spoon onto pie.

Toast coconut in frying pan or oven until golden. Cool. Sprinkle over topping. Yield: 1 pie.

COCONUT MERINGUE PIE: Use 3 egg yolks in Filling and make Meringue, page 66 with 3 egg whites. Spread over hot filling. Sprinkle with coconut. Bake in 350°F (180°C) oven about 10 minutes until golden.

PUMPKIN STREUSEL PIE

A real treat to have a wedge with a crunchy, sugary topping.

Canned pumpkin (or fresh, cooked and mashed), without spices	14 oz.	398 mL
Egg	1	1
Sweetened condensed milk (see Note)	11 oz.	300 mL
Chopped pecans or walnuts	1/3 cup	75 mL
Unbaked 9 inch (22 cm) pie shell, see page 140	1	1
STREUSEL TOPPING		
Brown sugar, packed	1/2 cup	125 mL
All-purpose flour	1/4 cup	60 mL
Butter or margarine	1/4 cup	60 mL
Cinnamon	1/2 tsp.	2 mL
Chopped pecans or walnuts	1/4 cup	60 mL

Beat first 3 ingredients together in bowl. Mix in pecans.

Pour into pie shell.

Streusel Topping: Mix first 4 ingredients until crumbly.

Add pecans. Stir. Sprinkle over pie. Bake on bottom shelf in 375°F (190°C) oven about 50 minutes until an inserted knife comes out clean. Cool. Yield: 1 pie.

Note: A 14 oz. (398 mL) can may also be used.

Two men with containers walking to the beach said they were mussel bound.

An attractive pie and a delight to bite into with fresh oranges in the filling.

Grated orange rind	1 tbsp.	15 mL
Juice from 2 oranges plus water to make	2 cups	450 mL
Lemon juice	1 tbsp.	15 mL
Granulated sugar	$3/4$ cup	175 mL
Cornstarch	$1/4$ cup	60 mL
Salt	$1/2$ tsp.	2 mL
Egg yolks	3	3
Butter or margarine, softened	2 tbsp.	30 mL
Orange, peeled, sectioned, membrane removed, cut in pieces	1	1
MERINGUE		
Egg whites, room temperature	3	3
Cream of tartar	$1/4$ tsp.	1 mL
Granulated sugar	6 tbsp.	100 mL
Baked 9 inch (22 cm) pie shell, see page 140	1	1

Finely grate orange rind. Set aside.

Heat orange juice, water and lemon juice in saucepan until it boils.

In small bowl stir sugar, cornstarch and salt. Add egg yolks and butter. Add orange rind. Beat with spoon to make smooth. Stir into boiling mixture. Boil until thickened.

Remove from heat. Stir in orange pieces. Set aside.

Meringue: Beat egg whites and cream of tartar in mixing bowl until a stiff froth. Gradually beat in sugar until stiff and sugar is dissolved.

Pour orange filling into pie shell. Spoon meringue over top sealing well to the crust all around. Bake in 350°F (180°C) oven about 10 minutes until golden. Cool. Yield: 1 pie.

BUTTERMILK PIE

A golden topped pie with a hint of nutmeg.

Eggs	3	3
Butter or margarine, melted	1/2 cup	125 mL
Granulated sugar	1 1/2 cups	375 mL
All-purpose flour	3 tbsp.	50 mL
Buttermilk	1 cup	250 mL
Vanilla	1 tsp.	5 mL
Lemon juice	1 tbsp.	15 mL
Nutmeg	1/8 tsp.	0.5 mL
Unbaked 9 inch (22 cm) pie shell, see page 140	1	1

Beat eggs in mixing bowl until frothy. Add butter, sugar and flour. Beat until smooth.

Stir in buttermilk, vanilla, lemon juice and nutmeg.

Pour into pie shell. Bake in 350°F (180°C) oven about 45 to 55 minutes until center is firm. Freezes well. Yield: 1 pie.

1. Creamy Peanut Butter Pie page 88
2. Chocolate Mocha Chiffon Pie page 23
3. French Silk Pie page 48
4. Turtle Pie page 13
5. Brownie Angel Pie page 130

FLAPPER PIE

One never tires of this old favorite cream pie.

GRAHAM CRACKER CRUST

Butter or margarine	$^1/_3$ cup	75 mL
Graham cracker crumbs	$1^1/_4$ cups	275 mL
Granulated sugar	$^1/_4$ cup	50 mL

FILLING

Milk	2 cups	450 mL
Granulated sugar	$^1/_2$ cup	125 mL
Cornstarch	$^1/_4$ cup	60 mL
Salt	$^1/_8$ tsp.	0.5 mL
Egg yolks	3	3
Milk	$^1/_4$ cup	60 mL
Vanilla	1 tsp.	5 mL

MERINGUE

Egg whites, room temperature	3	3
Cream of tartar	$^1/_4$ tsp.	1 mL
Granulated sugar	6 tbsp.	100 mL
Reserved crumbs	3 tbsp.	50 mL

Graham Cracker Crust: Melt butter in saucepan. Stir in graham crumbs and sugar. Reserve 3 tbsp. (50 mL). Press remaining crumbs into 9 inch (22 cm) pie plate covering sides and bottom. Bake in 350°F (180°C) oven for 10 minutes. Cool. To use this crust for other pies, do not reserve crumbs unless recipe directs.

Filling: Heat first amount of milk in heavy saucepan over medium heat until it boils.

Meanwhile mix sugar and cornstarch in bowl. Mix in salt, egg yolks, second amount of milk and vanilla. Stir into boiling milk until it returns to a boil and thickens. Pour into pie shell.

Meringue: Beat egg whites and cream of tartar in mixing bowl until a stiff froth. Add sugar gradually, beating until stiff and sugar is dissolved. Spread over pie sealing well to crust all around.

Sprinkle with reserved crumbs. Bake in 350°F (180°C) oven about 10 minutes until golden. Cool at least 2 to 3 hours. Yield: 1 pie.

CREAM PIE

A firm milk filling topped with meringue. An ancient type of pie still made today.

Milk	2¼ cups	500 mL
Granulated sugar	¾ cup	175 mL
All-purpose flour	½ cup	125 mL
Salt	½ tsp.	2 mL
Egg yolks	3	3
Vanilla	1 tsp.	5 mL
Milk	¼ cup	50 mL
Baked 9 inch (22 cm) pie shell, see page 140	1	1
MERINGUE		
Egg whites, room temperature	3	3
Cream of tartar	¼ tsp.	1 mL
Granulated sugar	6 tbsp.	100 mL

Heat first amount of milk in heavy saucepan until it simmers.

Meanwhile stir sugar, flour and salt together in bowl. Mix in egg yolks, vanilla and second amount of milk. Stir into simmering milk until it boils and thickens. Don't cook too long or it will curdle. If it does curdle, run through blender.

Pour into pie shell.

Meringue: Beat egg whites and cream of tartar until a firm froth. Gradually beat in sugar until stiff and sugar is dissolved. Pile on top of pie sealing to edges. Bake in 350°F (180°C) oven about 10 minutes until golden brown. Yield: 1 pie.

BANANA CREAM PIE: Add 2 sliced bananas to filling. Whipped Cream, page 30, may be used instead of meringue if desired.

Pictured on page 125.

MACADAMIA NUT PIE: Add ½ cup (125 mL) chopped macadamia nuts to filling. Cover with Whipped Cream, page 30.

A traditional Thanksgiving pie, but popular all year round.

Eggs	2	2
Brown sugar, packed (or white)	2/3 cup	150 mL
Canned pumpkin, without spices	14 oz.	398 mL
Cinnamon	3/4 tsp.	4 mL
Ginger	1/2 tsp.	2 mL
Nutmeg	1/2 tsp.	2 mL
Cloves	1/8 tsp.	0.5 mL
Salt	1/2 tsp.	2 mL
Milk (part or all evaporated is best)	1 1/2 cups	350 mL
Unbaked 9 inch (22 cm) pie shell, see page 140	1	1
Whipped Cream, see page 30		

Beat eggs lightly in mixing bowl. Add and mix next 8 ingredients in order given.

Pour into pie shell. If you have too much filling, cook in separate dish beside pie. Bake on bottom shelf in 450°F (230°C) oven for 10 minutes. Reduce heat to 350°F (180°C) and bake about 35 minutes until an inserted knife comes out clean. Cool.

Spread whipped cream over top. Yield: 1 pie.

A rich pie with a scrumptious caramel flavor. Garnish with whipped cream.

Brown sugar, or maple sugar, packed	1 1/2 cups	350 mL
All-purpose flour	1/4 cup	50 mL
Evaporated milk or whipping cream	1 1/2 cups	350 mL
Unbaked 9 inch (22 cm) pie shell, see page 140	1	1

Mix brown sugar and flour in bowl. Stir in milk.

Pour into pie shell. Bake on bottom shelf in 350°F (180°C) oven about 60 minutes. An inserted knife should come out fairly clean, but not quite completely. Yield: 1 pie.

Pictured on page 143.

PUMPKIN CHEESE PIE

An excellent variation. The cream cheese really adds to this pie.

Cream cheese, softened	4 oz.	125 g
Granulated sugar	1/4 cup	50 mL
Vanilla	1/2 tsp.	2 mL
Egg	1	1
Unbaked 9 inch (22 cm) pie shell, see page 140	1	1
Canned pumpkin (or fresh, cooked and sieved) without spices	14 oz.	398 mL
Eggs	2	2
Granulated sugar	1/2 cup	125 mL
Cinnamon	3/4 tsp.	4 mL
Nutmeg	1/4 tsp.	1 mL
Ginger	1/4 tsp.	1 mL
Salt	1/4 tsp.	1 mL
Evaporated milk	1 cup	250 mL

Beat cream cheese, first amount of sugar, vanilla and 1 egg until smooth in small mixing bowl.

Spread over bottom of pie shell.

Mix pumpkin and 2 eggs well. Add second amount of sugar, spices and salt. Stir. Add milk. Stir. Pour over cheese layer. If there is too much filling cook the extra in a small container beside the pie. Bake on bottom rack in 350°F (180°C) oven about 1 hour until an inserted knife comes out clean. Cool. Yield: 1 pie.

Double names seem to be the trend now. Ferdinand and Liza had a new baby and called him Ferdiliza.

LEMON CREAM PIE

A good lemon flavor to this. Contains sour cream.

Granulated sugar	1 cup	250 mL
Cornstarch	1/4 cup	60 mL
Butter or margarine	2 tbsp.	30 mL
Lemon juice	1/4 cup	60 mL
Grated lemon rind	1 tbsp.	15 mL
Milk	1 cup	225 mL
Egg, beaten	1	1
Sour cream	1 cup	225 mL
Baked 9 inch (22 cm) pie shell, see page 140	1	1

Whipped Cream, see page 30

In heavy saucepan mix sugar and cornstarch. Add butter, lemon juice, lemon rind and milk. Heat and stir over medium heat until it boils and thickens.

Stir about 1/4 cup (50 mL) mixture into egg then stir egg mixture back into saucepan. Stir and return to a boil. Remove from heat. Cool.

Add sour cream. Stir and pour into pie shell. Chill.

Cover pie with whipped cream. Yield: 1 pie.

BLUEBERRY SAUCE

Try this over a lemon flavored pie.

Blueberries, fresh or frozen	1 1/2 cups	375 mL
Granulated sugar	1/3 cup	75 mL
Lemon juice	1 tsp.	5 mL
Cornstarch	1 tbsp.	15 mL
Water	1 tbsp.	15 mL

Stir blueberries, sugar and lemon juice together in saucepan. Place over low heat until berries release some juice. Bring to a boil.

Mix cornstarch and water in small cup. Stir into boiling berries until mixture thickens and is clear. Cool. Spoon over wedges of pie. Lemon or vanilla flavored pies are good choices. Makes about 1 cup (250 mL).

CARAMEL SAUCE

This finishing touch can be stored in the refrigerator and warmed when needed.

Granulated sugar	¹/₂ cup	125 mL
Water	¹/₂ cup	125 mL
Granulated sugar	¹/₂ cup	125 mL
Whipping cream	¹/₃ cup	75 mL
Vanilla	1 tsp.	5 mL

Place first amount of sugar in heavy frying pan over medium-low heat. Stir continually as it melts and turns a coppery-brown. Remove from heat.

Add water and stir. It will spatter at first. Return to heat and stir until mixed.

Stir in remaining sugar, cream and vanilla. Serve warm over cream or custard pies or any cake-like pie. Makes about 1 cup (250 mL).

CUSTARD SAUCE

A thin custard, strained for smoothness. A good topper.

Milk	1 cup	225 mL
Granulated sugar	3 tbsp.	50 mL
All-purpose flour	1 tsp.	5 mL
Eggs	2	2
Vanilla	¹/₂ tsp.	2 mL
Brandy flavoring (optional)	¹/₂ tsp.	2 mL

Heat milk in double boiler.

In small bowl mix sugar, flour and eggs well. Stir into hot milk until it thickens slightly. Remove from heat.

Add vanilla and brandy flavoring. Strain. Serve hot or cold over warm fruit pie or any pie you would like to serve with a sauce. Makes about 1¹/₂ cups (375 mL).

LEMON CHEESE

These treats may be assembled any time as long as you have baked tart shells on hand. Small shells work well.

Eggs	3	3
Juice of lemons	3	3
Granulated sugar	1 cup	250 mL
Butter or margarine	3 tbsp.	50 mL

Beat eggs well in top of double boiler. Some aluminum pans will darken lemon. Use stainless steel or coated pan if possible. Mix in lemon juice, sugar and butter. Cook over boiling water about 15 minutes until smooth and thickened. Stir continually. Mixture should mound when ready. It will thicken more when chilled. Remove from heat. Cool. Store in jars in refrigerator or freeze. Makes about 1 ¼ cups (275 mL).

LEMON CHEESE TARTS: Spoon filling into a few baked tart shells, page 140. Top with cherry or dab of whipped cream.

Pictured on page 125.

TWO STEP MERINGUE

This makes a golden high topping. No weeping allowed.

Cornstarch	1 tbsp.	15 mL
Water	½ cup	125 mL
Egg whites, room temperature	3	3
Salt, light sprinkle		
Granulated sugar	6 tbsp.	100 mL
Vanilla	½ tsp.	2 mL

In small saucepan mix water and cornstarch. Heat and stir until it boils and thickens. Cool thoroughly. You can hasten cooling by placing pan in cold water.

Beat egg whites and salt until a stiff froth. Add sugar gradually, beating until stiff and sugar is dissolved. Add vanilla and cornstarch mixture. Beat until mixed and stiff. Spread over pie sealing to edges. If not sealed very well, meringue will shrink when cool. Bake in 350°F (180°C) oven about 10 minutes until golden. Cool away from drafts. Yield: 1 meringue topping.

MILE HIGH PIE

A snap to make. You can cut and eat this frozen pie directly from the freezer. Great to have on hand. A chocolate crumb crust is a pretty contrast to try second time around.

SHORT NUT CRUST

All-purpose flour	1 cup	250 mL
Granulated sugar	3 tbsp.	50 mL
Butter or margarine, softened	1/2 cup	125 mL
Finely chopped walnuts	1/3 cup	75 mL

FILLING

Egg whites	2	2
Lemon juice	2 tbsp.	30 mL
Granulated sugar	1 cup	225 mL
Frozen sliced strawberries in heavy syrup, almost thawed	15 oz.	425 g
Whipping cream (or 1 envelope topping)	1 cup	250 mL

Short Nut Crust: Combine flour, sugar and butter in bowl. Work together until it forms a ball.

Add walnuts and work in. Press evenly onto bottom and sides of 9 inch (22 cm) pie plate. Prick bottom with fork tines. Bake in 350°F (180°C) oven about 20 minutes until lightly browned. Cool.

Filling: Place egg whites, lemon juice, sugar and strawberries in mixing bowl. Beat on high speed about 10 to 15 minutes until thickened and volume has greatly increased. It should be stiff.

Beat cream in small mixing bowl until stiff. Fold into strawberry mixture. Pile into pie shell. Freeze. This needn't be taken out of freezer until you are ready to use it. It cuts easily while frozen. Yield: 1 pie.

The real reason for long summer days and short winter days is that heat expands and cold contracts.

A crispy chocolate crust holds this frozen strawberry cream pie. A vanilla wafer crust suits this pie as well.

Chocolate Crisp Crust, see page 82	1	1
FILLING		
Frozen sliced strawberries or raspberries in heavy syrup, thawed and drained	15 oz.	425 g
Vanilla ice cream, softened	3 cups	700 mL

Prepare crust and freeze.

Filling: In large bowl stir strawberries and ice cream together well. It doesn't need to be completely mixed. Pour into pie shell. Freeze. Yield: 1 pie.

LAYERED FUDGE FROST

A super pie. Vanilla ice cream is layered with just the right amount of chocolate. Easy to cut while frozen.

CHOCOLATE SAUCE		
Evaporated milk	1 cup	250 mL
Semisweet chocolate chips	1 cup	250 mL
Tiny marshmallows	1 cup	250 mL
FILLING		
Vanilla ice cream, softened	1 qt.	1 L
Baked 9 inch (22 cm) pie shell, see page 140	1	1
Chopped pecans or walnuts	2 tbsp.	30 mL

Chocolate Sauce: Pour evaporated milk and chocolate chips into saucepan over medium-low heat. Stir often until chips are melted.

Add marshmallows. Stir until melted. Cool.

Filling: Stir ½ of ice cream and spread in pie shell. Freeze. Spread ½ chocolate sauce over top. Freeze. Repeat.

Sprinkle with pecans. Keep frozen. Yield: 1 pie.

FROZEN HAWAIIAN PIE

Mashed banana is the subtle flavor in this pie. With a taste of Hawaii.

Tiny marshmallows	2 cups	500 mL
Canned crushed pineapple with juice	14 oz.	398 mL
Grated lemon rind	1/2 tsp.	2 mL
Medium banana, mashed	1	1
Lemon juice	1 1/2 tsp.	7 mL
Whipping cream (or 1 envelope topping)	1 cup	250 mL
Baked Graham Cracker Crust, see page 73	1	1

In medium heavy saucepan combine marshmallows, pineapple with juice and lemon rind. Place over medium-low heat. Stir often as marshmallows melt. Chill well, stirring occasionally until thickened.

Stir in banana and lemon juice.

Beat cream in small mixing bowl until stiff. Fold into pineapple-banana mixture.

Pour into pie shell. Freeze uncovered. Cover and store in freezer. Remove from freezer and leave at room temperature at least 30 minutes before cutting. Yield: 1 pie.

Pictured on page 35.

CHOCO MINT PIE

Chocolate and mint are meant for each other. A frozen duo.

CHOCOLATE CRISP CRUST		
Butter or margarine	2 tbsp.	30 mL
Semisweet chocolate chips	2/3 cup	150 mL
Crisp rice cereal	2 cups	450 mL
FILLING		
Chocolate ice cream	1 qt.	1 L
Crème de menthe, (or 1 tsp., 5 mL, peppermint flavoring)	1/3 cup	75 mL
Chocolate Sauce, see page 81		

(continued on next page)

Chocolate Crisp Crust: Melt butter and chocolate chips in medium saucepan over low heat. Stir often to hasten melting. Remove from heat. Add cereal. Stir to coat. Press onto bottom and sides of 9 inch (22 cm) pie plate. Freeze.

Filling: Soften ice cream so you can stir in crème de menthe. Spoon into pie shell. Freeze. Cover to store.

Spoon Chocolate Sauce over each serving. Yield: 1 pie.

FROZEN CHOCOLATE PIE

Nutty with a whipped smooth texture.

Baked Graham Cracker Crust, see page 73, or Chocolate Cookie Crust, see page 29	1	1
FILLING		
Cream cheese, softened	8 oz.	250 g
Granulated sugar	1 cup	250 mL
Salt	$1/4$ tsp.	1 mL
Vanilla	1 tsp.	5 mL
Semisweet chocolate chips	1 cup	250 mL
Milk	$1/3$ cup	75 mL
Whipping cream (or 1 envelope topping)	1 cup	250 mL
Chopped pecans or walnuts	$1/2$ cup	125 mL

Prepare pie shell. Cool.

Filling: Combine first 4 ingredients in bowl. Beat until smooth.

Heat chocolate chips and milk in small saucepan over low heat until melted. Stir often. Cool. Place saucepan in cold water to hasten cooling. Beat into cream cheese mixture.

Beat cream in small bowl until stiff. Fold in.

Add pecans and fold in. Turn into pie shell. Freeze. Serve plain or topped with Whipped Cream, page 30, or Chocolate Sauce, page 81. Yield: 1 pie.

BAKED ALASKA PIE

A flamboyant finale with a soft marshmallow-textured meringue. A regular meringue may also be used.

CHOCOLATE GRAHAM CRUST

Butter or margarine	⅓ cup	75 mL
Graham cracker crumbs	1 cup	250 mL
Granulated sugar	¼ cup	60 mL
Cocoa	3 tbsp.	50 mL

FILLING

Strawberry ice cream, softened	1 qt.	1 L

COATING

Granulated sugar	1 cup	225 mL
Water	⅓ cup	75 mL
Cream of tartar	¼ tsp.	1 mL
Vanilla	1 tsp.	5 mL
Egg whites	2	2

Chocolate Graham Cracker Crust: Melt butter in saucepan. Add crumbs, sugar and cocoa. Stir. Press in bottom and sides of ungreased 9 inch (22 cm) pie plate. Freeze.

Filling: Fill pie shell with softened ice cream. Smooth top and freeze.

Coating: Preheat oven to 500°F (260°C). Measure sugar, water, cream of tartar and vanilla into saucepan. Stir and bring to a boil. Dissolve sugar.

Put egg whites in large bowl. Pour hot mixture very slowly over egg whites as you begin beating. Beat about 4 minutes until stiff peaks form. Cover ice cream right to edge of crust. At this point pie can be returned to freezer. Bake meringue-topped pie for 3 to 4 minutes until browned. Serve immediately. Yield: 1 pie.

FRUIT ALASKA: Drained fruit such as crushed pineapple, or sweetened strawberries or raspberries may be stirred into ice cream, spread in pastry shell, then frozen. Proceed with meringue. Yield: 1 pie.

BLUEBERRY ALASKA: Line 8 inch (20 cm) pie plate with plastic wrap. Fill with layer of softened ice cream about ¾ to 1 inch (2 to 2.5 cm) thick. Freeze. Make Meringue, page 44. Unwrap ice cream and place over blueberry pie (or other kind) which has been brought to room temperature. Quickly cover completely with meringue sealing to edge of crust. Bake in 500°F (260°C) oven 3 to 4 minutes to brown. Serve. A real dress-up for pies. Yield: 1 pie.

FROSTY LIME PIE

A refreshing dessert to have in the freezer for barbecue days.

CHOCOLATE GRAHAM CRUST

Butter or margarine	¹/₃ cup	75 mL
Graham cracker crumbs	1¹/₄ cups	275 mL
Granulated sugar	¹/₄ cup	60 mL
Cocoa	3 tbsp.	50 mL

FILLING

Cream cheese, softened	8 oz.	250 g
Granulated sugar	¹/₂ cup	125 mL
Egg yolk	1	1
Lime juice	¹/₂ cup	125 mL
Grated lime rind (optional)	1 tsp.	5 mL
Egg white, room temperature	1	1
Whipping cream (or 1 envelope topping)	1 cup	250 mL
Drops of green food color	2-4	2-4

Chocolate Graham Crust: Melt butter in saucepan. Stir in graham crumbs, sugar and cocoa. Press evenly on bottom and sides of 9 inch (22 cm) pie plate. Bake in 350°F (180°C) oven for 10 minutes. Cool.

Filling: Beat cream cheese and sugar until smooth. Beat in egg yolk. Add lime juice and rind. Mix in slowly.

Beat egg white with clean beater until stiff. Fold in.

Using same beaters and bowl beat cream until stiff. Fold in. Add a few drops of food coloring to tint a pale green if desired. Freeze. Cut 15 minutes before serving. Yield: 1 pie.

The football stadium is usually filled to capacity. So are some of the fans.

MUD PIE

A universally popular frozen pie. Chocolate sauce tops it off for an extra touch.

COOKIE CRUST		
Butter or margarine	1/2 cup	125 mL
Chocolate wafer crumbs	2 cups	500 mL
FILLING		
Coffee ice cream, softened	1 qt.	1 L
TOPPING		
Semisweet chocolate chips	2/3 cup	150 mL
Corn syrup	2 tbsp.	30 mL
Butter or margarine	1 tbsp.	15 mL
Whipping cream	1/4 cup	50 mL
Instant coffee granules	1 tsp.	5 mL
Hot water	2 tsp.	10 mL
GARNISH		
Whipping cream (or 1 envelope topping)	1 cup	250 mL
Granulated sugar	2 tsp.	10 mL
Vanilla	1/2 tsp.	2 mL
Semisweet baking chocolate square, shaved	1 × 1 oz.	1 × 28 g
Toasted sliced almonds	2 tbsp.	30 mL

Chocolate Sauce, see page 81

Cookie Crust: Melt butter in saucepan. Stir in crumbs. Press onto bottom and sides of 9 inch (22 cm) pie plate. Bake in 350°F (180°C) oven for 10 minutes. Cool.

Filling: Stir ice cream in bowl to soften slightly. Spread carefully in pie crust. Freeze until firm.

Topping: Combine first 4 ingredients in saucepan over medium-low heat. Stir often to hasten melting of chocolate chips.

Dissolve coffee granules in hot water. Add to saucepan. Stir. Remove from heat. Cool. Spread over ice cream. Return to freezer.

Garnish: To serve, beat cream, sugar and vanilla in small mixing bowl until stiff. Spoon onto pie around edge.

(continued on next page)

Garnish with shaved chocolate and toasted almonds on whipped cream around edge.

Spoon chocolate sauce over each wedge. Yield: 1 pie.

Note: If coffee ice cream is not available dissolve 2 tsp. (10 mL) instant coffee granules in 4 tsp. (20 mL) hot water. Mix into softened vanilla ice cream.

FROZEN LEMON PIE

White frosty citrus pie. A real treat.

VANILLA WAFER CRUST

Butter or margarine	⅓ cup	75 mL
Vanilla wafer crumbs	1¼ cups	275 mL
Granulated sugar	2 tbsp.	30 mL

FILLING

Egg whites, room temperature	2	2
Granulated sugar	⅔ cup	150 mL
Lemon juice	¼ cup	60 mL
Whipping cream (or 1 envelope topping)	1 cup	250 mL
Reserved crumbs	2 tbsp.	30 mL

Vanilla Wafer Crust: Melt butter in small saucepan over medium heat. Stir in wafer crumbs and sugar. Reserve ¼ cup (60 mL). Press remaining crumbs evenly onto bottom and sides of 9 inch (22 cm) pie plate. Bake in 350°F (180°C) oven about 10 to 15 minutes until browned. Cool.

Filling: Beat egg whites in small mixing bowl until soft peaks form. Gradually add sugar beating until stiff. Beat in lemon juice.

Beat cream in small bowl until stiff. Fold into egg white mixture. Turn into pie shell.

Sprinkle with reserved crumbs. Freeze, then cover and store in freezer. Remove 20 to 30 minutes before serving. For a special treat serve with Blueberry Sauce, page 77. Yield: 1 pie.

CREAMY PEANUT BUTTER PIE

A velvety filling in a chocolate crumb crust. Peanut butter flavor is mild. A frozen confection.

Cream cheese, softened	8 oz.	250 g
Icing (confectioner's) sugar	1 cup	250 mL
Smooth peanut butter	³/₄ cup	175 mL
Milk	¹/₂ cup	125 mL
Vanilla	1 tsp.	5 mL
Whipping Cream (or 1 envelope topping)	1 cup	250 mL
Chocolate Graham Crust, see page 85	1	1
Finely chopped peanuts	1 tbsp.	15 mL

Beat cream cheese, icing sugar and peanut butter in bowl until smooth.

Slowly beat in milk and vanilla.

Beat cream until stiff. Fold in.

Turn into pie shell. Sprinkle with peanuts. Chill. This may be served when chilled well although it is not too firm. Freeze for best results. Can be cut immediately upon removal from freezer. Yield: 1 pie.

Pictured on page 71.

1. Jam Tarts (Raspberry) page 146
2. Jam Tarts (Apricot) page 146
3. Orange Chiffon Pie page 39
4. Light Strawberry Pie page 32
5. Grasshopper Pie page 42

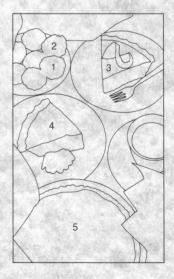

A frosty delight on a gingersnap crust.

GINGERSNAP CRUST		
Butter or margarine	1/3 cup	75 mL
Gingersnap crumbs	1 1/4 cups	275 mL
Granulated sugar	2 tbsp.	30 mL
FILLING		
Canned pumpkin, without spices	1 cup	250 mL
Brown sugar	1/2 cup	125 mL
Cinnamon	1/2 tsp.	2 mL
Ginger	1/2 tsp.	2 mL
Nutmeg	1/4 tsp.	1 mL
Salt	1/4 tsp.	1 mL
Whipping cream (or 1 envelope topping)	1 cup	250 mL
Vanilla ice cream, softened slightly	4 cups	1 L

Gingersnap Crust: Melt butter in saucepan. Stir in gingersnap crumbs and sugar. Press onto bottom and sides of 9 inch (22 cm) pie plate. Chill.

Filling: Mix first 6 ingredients well in large bowl.

Beat cream until stiff. Set aside.

Stir ice cream into pumpkin mixture. Fold in whipped cream. Turn into pie shell. Freeze. Let stand 15 minutes before serving. Yield: 1 pie.

There was a time when something you got for nothing didn't cost so much.

PIÑA COLADA PIE

Smooth, mellow and absolutely yummy.

Baked Shortbread Crust, 9 inch (22 cm), see page 24	1	1
Cream cheese, softened	8 oz.	250 g
Granulated sugar	1/2 cup	125 mL
Rum flavoring	1 tsp.	5 mL
Crushed pineapple, drained	14 oz.	398 mL
Corn syrup	1/4 cup	60 mL
Coconut flavoring	1 tsp.	5 mL
Whipping cream (or 1 envelope topping)	1 cup	250 mL
Whipped Cream, see page 30, make 1/2 recipe		
Maraschino cherries	6	6

Prepare pie shell. Cool.

Beat cream cheese, sugar and rum flavoring together until smooth.

Stir in pineapple, syrup and coconut flavoring.

Beat cream until stiff. Fold into cheese mixture. Turn into pie shell. Freeze.

To serve, top each wedge with a dollop of whipped cream and a cherry. Yield: 1 pie.

Pictured on page 35.

ICED LEMONADE PIE

A pretty pink frozen pie with a refreshing flavor. Resembles a sherbet.

Frozen concentrated pink lemonade (or yellow), thawed	6 1/4 oz.	178 mL
Vanilla ice cream	4 cups	1 L
Drops of red food color	2 - 4	2 - 4
Baked Graham Cracker Crust, see page 73, reserve 2 tbsp. (30 mL) for topping	1	1

(continued on next page)

Mix lemonade and ice cream thoroughly. Add food coloring to make a pleasing light pink if using pink lemonade. If using regular lemonade, use a few drops of yellow food coloring.

Pour into pie shell. Sprinkle with reserved crumbs. Freeze. Yield: 1 pie.

DUTCH APPLE PIE

Apple pie with a streusel topping. Glaze is optional. It's good both ways.

Cooking apples, peeled, cored and cut up	**2 lbs.**	**900 g**
Granulated sugar	**2/3 cup**	**150 mL**
Brown sugar, packed	**1/3 cup**	**75 mL**
All-purpose flour	**2 tbsp.**	**30 mL**
Cinnamon	**1/2 tsp.**	**2 mL**
Unbaked 9 inch (22 cm) pie shell, see page 140	**1**	**1**
TOPPING		
All-purpose flour	**2/3 cup**	**150 mL**
Brown sugar, packed	**6 tbsp.**	**100 mL**
Butter or margarine	**1/4 cup**	**60 mL**
Cinnamon	**1/4 tsp.**	**1 mL**
Salt	**1/4 tsp.**	**1 mL**
GLAZE (optional)		
Icing (confectioner's) sugar	**1/2 cup**	**125 mL**
Lemon juice	**1-2 tbsp.**	**15-30 mL**

Quarter apples. Cut each quarter in half lengthwise then cut twice crosswise into large bowl. You will need 5 cups (1.12 L).

Add next 4 ingredients and toss.

Pour into pie shell.

Topping: Combine flour, sugar, butter, cinnamon and salt. Mix until crumbly. Sprinkle over pie. Bake on bottom shelf in 400°F (200°C) oven for 10 minutes. Turn oven to 325°F (160°C) and bake about 50 minutes until apples are tender. Cool.

Glaze: Glaze is optional. Mix icing sugar and lemon juice to make a barely pourable glaze. Drizzle over pie shortly before serving. Yield: 1 pie.

Pictured on page 53.

BLUEBERRY PIE

Serve warm with ice cream or cold with whipped cream or cheese. A favorite berry filling.

Pastry for a 2 crust pie, see page 140

Granulated sugar	1 cup	250 mL
All-purpose flour	1/4 cup	60 mL
Blueberries	4 cups	900 mL
Lemon juice	1 tbsp.	15 mL
Granulated sugar	1/4-1/2 tsp.	1-2 mL

Roll pastry and line 9 inch (22 cm) pie plate. Roll top crust.

In large bowl stir first amount of sugar, flour and blueberries together until mixed well. Let stand 10 minutes. Pour into pie shell.

Drizzle with lemon juice. Dampen pastry edges. Cover with second crust. Trim and crimp to seal. Cut vents in top.

Sprinkle with remaining sugar. Bake on bottom shelf in 350°F (180°C) oven about 45 minutes until cooked and browned. Yield: 1 pie.

SASKATOON PIE: Use saskatoons instead of blueberries.

RAISIN SOUR CREAM PIE

A pleasant tang to this pie but you can't tell it's from sour cream.

Granulated sugar	3/4 cup	175 mL
All-purpose flour	2 tbsp.	30 mL
Salt	1/4 tsp.	1 mL
Eggs	2	2
Sour cream	1 1/2 cups	375 mL
Raisins	1 cup	250 mL
Lemon juice	2 tbsp.	30 mL
Baked 9 inch (22 cm) pie shell, see page 140	1	1

WHIPPED CREAM

Whipping cream (or 1 envelope topping)	1 cup	250 mL
Granulated sugar	2 tsp.	10 mL
Vanilla	1/2 tsp.	2 mL

(continued on next page)

Stir sugar, flour and salt together in heavy saucepan. A double boiler may be used instead.

Mix in eggs. Add sour cream, raisins and lemon juice. Heat and stir until it boils and thickens.

Pour into pastry shell. Cool.

Whipped Cream: Beat cream, sugar and vanilla in small bowl until stiff. Spread over pie. Chill. Yield: 1 pie.

CONCORD GRAPE PIE

Grape skins actually taste good in this pie.

Pastry for a 2 crust pie, see page 140

Concord grapes, about 2 lbs. (900 g)	5 cups	1.12 L
Granulated sugar	1 cup	225 mL
All-purpose flour	1/3 cup	75 mL
Grape skins		
Seeded grape pulp		
Salt	1/4 tsp.	1 mL
Lemon juice	2 tsp.	10 mL
Granulated sugar	1/4-1/2 tsp.	1-2 mL

Roll pastry and line 9 inch (22 cm) pie plate. Roll top crust. Cover with plastic to keep moist.

Slip skins from grapes. Place skins in small bowl and place pulp in medium saucepan. Bring pulp to a boil. Cover and cook slowly about 10 minutes until soft. Put through food mill or sieve to remove seeds.

In medium bowl stir first amount of sugar and flour. Add grape skins, pulp, salt and lemon juice. Mix well. Pour into pie shell. Dampen edges. Place top crust in position. Trim and flute to seal. Cut vents in top.

Sprinkle with remaining sugar. Bake on bottom rack of 350°F (180°C) oven about 50 minutes until browned and cooked. Yield: 1 pie.

GOOSEBERRY PIE

Quite an uncommon pie. Next time you find this fruit, be sure to try it.

Gooseberries	3¹/₂ cups	800 mL
Granulated sugar	1¹/₂ cups	350 mL
Minute tapioca	3 tbsp.	45 mL
Pastry for a 2 crust pie, see page 140		
Granulated sugar	¹/₄ -¹/₂ tsp.	1-2 mL

Combine gooseberries, first amount of sugar and tapioca in large bowl. Stir. Let stand 15 minutes.

Roll pastry and line 9 inch (22 cm) pie plate. Pour in gooseberry mixture. Roll top crust. Dampen pastry rim. Cover with crust. Trim and crimp to seal. Cut slits in top.

Sprinkle with remaining sugar. Bake on bottom shelf in 350°F (180°C) oven about 45 minutes until browned and fruit is tender. Yield: 1 pie.

DEEP APPLE PIE

Any fruit may be made into a deep pie. Just use more fruit and sugar than for a regular pie. Add a top crust and bake.

Pastry to cover casserole, see page 140		
Cooking apples, peeled, cored and cut up	3 lbs.	1.36 kg
Granulated sugar	1¹/₄ cups	275 mL
Cinnamon	¹/₂ tsp.	2 mL
Lemon juice (optional)	1 tbsp.	15 mL
Vanilla (optional)	1 tsp.	5 mL
Granulated sugar	¹/₄ -¹/₂ tsp.	1-2 mL
Cinnamon	¹/₂ tsp.	2 mL

Roll pastry ¹/₈ inch (3 mm) thick. Cut about 1 inch (2.5 cm) larger all around than casserole dish.

Place apples in 3 quart (4 L) casserole. Pour first amount of sugar over apples. Sprinkle with cinnamon. If you want juice to be thicker, stir 2 tbsp. (30 mL) all-purpose flour into sugar before pouring over apples.

(continued on next page)

Mix lemon juice and vanilla in small cup. Drizzle over pie. Place pastry over all, so it comes up a bit on the sides and buckles somewhat on top. Cut slits for steam to escape.

Sprinkle with remaining sugar. Bake in 350°F (180°C) oven about 45 to 55 minutes until apples are tender and crust is browned. Serves 8.

PARTY PEACH PIE

You can't imagine how good this is without trying it. The small amount of blackberries or raspberries is truly an enhancement.

Pastry for a 2 crust pie, see page 140

Granulated sugar	**³/₄ cup**	**175 mL**
All-purpose flour	**¹/₂ cup**	**125 mL**
Peeled and sliced peaches	**3 cups**	**700 mL**
Blackberries, fresh or loosely frozen	**1 cup**	**250 mL**
Granulated sugar	**¹/₄-¹/₂ tsp.**	**1-2 mL**

Roll pastry and line 9 inch (22 cm) pie plate. Roll top crust.

In large bowl combine first amount of sugar and flour. Stir well.

Dip peaches in boiling water for 1 minute. Run cold water over them. Peel and slice. Add peaches and blackberries to sugar mixture. Toss together. Pour into pie shell. Dampen crust edges. Place pastry over top. Trim and crimp to seal. Cut slits in top.

Sprinkle with remaining sugar. Bake on bottom shelf in 350°F (180°C) oven about 45 minutes until browned and peaches are tender. Yield: 1 pie.

Note: Raspberries may be substituted for blackberries if necessary.

Paré Pointer

The necklace told the hat to go on ahead while it would hang around.

PEACH PIE

Both this and the variation are good. To decide on your favorite try each one.

Granulated sugar	1 cup	250 mL
All-purpose flour	1/3 cup	75 mL
Peeled and sliced peaches	5 cups	1.13 L
Pastry for a 2 crust pie, see page 140		
Granulated sugar	1/4-1/2 tsp.	1-2 mL

In large bowl combine first 2 ingredients. Stir.

Place peaches in boiling water for 1 minute. Remove and drop into cold water. Peel and slice. Add peaches to sugar mixture. Stir well.

Roll pastry and line 9 inch (22 cm) pie plate. Fill with peach mixture. Dampen edges. Roll top crust. Cover pie. Trim and seal. Cut vents in top.

Sprinkle with remaining sugar. Bake on bottom shelf in 425°F (220°C) oven for 10 minutes. Lower heat to 350°F (180°C) and bake about 40 minutes until browned and fruit is cooked. Yield: 1 pie.

Variation: Use half brown sugar and half granulated. Add 1/2 tsp. (2 mL) cinnamon. A delicious variation.

RAISIN PIE

Another family favorite. Saucy delicious.

Raisins	2 cups	500 mL
Water	1 cup	250 mL
Brown sugar, packed	1 cup	250 mL
All-purpose flour	1/4 cup	60 mL
Salt	1/4 tsp.	1 mL
Lemon juice	2 tbsp.	30 mL
Grated lemon rind (optional)	1 tsp.	5 mL
Pastry for a 2 crust pie, see page 140		
Granulated sugar	1/4-1/2 tsp.	1-2 mL

(continued on next page)

Combine raisins and water in saucepan. Bring to a boil. Cover and simmer slowly for 5 minutes.

In small bowl stir brown sugar, flour and salt together. Stir into simmering raisins until it returns to a boil and thickens. Remove from heat.

Add lemon juice and rind. Cool 1/2 hour or so.

Roll pastry and line 9 inch (22 cm) pie plate. Pour raisin filling into shell. Dampen edge. Roll another crust and put over top. Trim and crimp to seal. Cut vents in top.

Sprinkle with granulated sugar. Bake on bottom shelf in 400°F (200°C) oven about 30 minutes until browned. Yield: 1 pie.

PINEAPPLE PIE

A double crust pie using canned pineapple.

Crushed pineapple with juice	**19 oz.**	**540 mL**
Granulated sugar	**3/4 cup**	**175 mL**
Lemon juice	**1 tbsp.**	**15 mL**
Cornstarch	**3 tbsp.**	**50 mL**
Pastry for a 2 crust pie, see page 140		
Granulated sugar	**1/4-1/2 tsp.**	**1-2 mL**
Whipped Cream, see page 30		

Place first 4 ingredients in saucepan. Stir thoroughly to blend cornstarch. Heat and stir until it boils for 1 minute and thickens. Cool until warm.

Roll pastry and line 9 inch (22 cm) pie plate. Roll top crust. Pour filling into pie shell. Dampen edges of pastry. Place crust on top. Trim and crimp to seal. Cut vents in top.

Sprinkle with remaining sugar. Bake on bottom shelf in 400°F (200°C) oven about 30 to 35 minutes until browned. Cool.

Serve with dollops of whipped cream. Yield: 1 pie.

CORAL REEF PIE

A pretty yellow and pink pie. Excellent flavor.

Crushed pineapple with juice	19 oz.	540 mL
Granulated sugar	¼ cup	50 mL
Cornstarch	2 tbsp.	30 mL
Water	¼ cup	50 mL
Egg yolks, beaten	2	2
Butter or margarine, softened	1 tbsp.	15 mL
Baked 9 inch (22 cm) pie shell, see page 140	1	1
COCONUT TOPPING		
Egg whites, room temperature	2	2
Cream of tartar	¼ tsp.	1 mL
Salt, just a few grains		
Granulated sugar	½ cup	125 mL
Drops of red food color	4-5	4-5
Thread coconut	½ cup	125 mL

Heat pineapple with juice and sugar in saucepan until it boils.

Stir cornstarch into water. Add to pineapple stirring until thickened.

Mix egg yolks and butter in small bowl. Stir about ½ cup (125 mL) hot mixture into egg yolk mixture. Now stir egg yolk mixture back into saucepan. Bring to a boil.

Pour into pie shell.

Coconut Topping: Beat egg whites, cream of tartar and salt in small mixing bowl until a stiff froth. Add sugar gradually, beating until stiff and sugar is dissolved.

Fold in food coloring and coconut. Spread over pie, sealing well to crust all around. Bake in 325°F (160°C) oven about 30 minutes until browned. Yield: 1 pie.

Pictured on page 35.

Pare Pointer

Cruel cooks beat eggs and whip cream.

SOUR CREAM DATE PIE

It's time to try dates in a pie. Flavorful.

Sour cream	1¹/₂ cups	350 mL
Granulated sugar	³/₄ cup	175 mL
Cornstarch	3 tbsp.	50 mL
Egg yolks	3	3
Cinnamon	1 tsp.	5 mL
Chopped dates	1 cup	250 mL
Chopped walnuts	¹/₂ cup	125 mL
Vanilla	¹/₂ tsp.	2 mL
Baked 9 inch (22 cm) pie shell, see page 140	1	1
MERINGUE		
Egg whites, room temperature	3	3
Cream of tartar	¹/₄ tsp.	1 mL
Granulated sugar	6 tbsp.	100 mL

Measure first 5 ingredients into heavy saucepan. Cook until thick, stirring continuously.

Add dates. Remove from heat. Let stand 15 minutes for dates to soften.

Add walnuts and vanilla. Stir.

Pour into pie shell.

Meringue: Beat egg whites and cream of tartar in bowl until a stiff froth. Beat in sugar gradually until stiff and sugar is dissolved. Spread over pie sealing well up to edge all around. Bake in 350°F (180°C) oven about 10 minutes until lightly browned. Yield: 1 pie.

Pictured on page 143.

Paré Pointer

The reason toadstools look like umbrellas is that they grow in wet places.

CANNED PEAR PIE

You will be hard pressed to distinguish this from fresh pears.

Granulated sugar	1 cup	225 mL
All-purpose flour	2 tbsp.	30 mL
Lemon juice	1/4 cup	50 mL
Reserved juice from pears	1/3 cup	75 mL
Egg, beaten	1	1
Pastry for a 2 crust pie, see page 140		
Canned pears, drained and cubed	2 x 14 oz.	2 x 398 mL
Granulated sugar	1/4-1/2 tsp.	1-2 mL

Measure first amount of sugar and flour into saucepan. Stir well. Mix in lemon juice, pear juice and egg. Heat and stir until it boils and thickens. Remove from heat. Cool by setting saucepan in cold water for 5 minutes.

Roll pastry. Line 9 inch (22 cm) pie plate. Roll top crust.

Place pears in pie shell. Pour thickened mixture over top. Dampen edges of crust. Cover with top pastry. Trim and crimp to seal. Cut vents in top.

Sprinkle with remaining sugar. Bake on bottom shelf in 400°F (200°C) oven about 35 minutes until browned. Yield: 1 pie.

APPLE RAISIN PIE

Two of the most common pie ingredients combine to make a delicious pie.

Pastry for a 2 crust pie, see page 140		
Granulated sugar	1 cup	250 mL
All-purpose flour	3 tbsp.	50 mL
Cinnamon	1/2 tsp.	2 mL
Cooking apples, peeled, cored and cut up	5 cups	1.12 L
Dark raisins	1/2 cup	125 mL
Whipping cream	1/2 cup	125 mL
Granulated sugar	1/4-1/2 tsp.	1-2 mL

(continued on next page)

Roll out pastry and line a 9 inch (22 cm) pie plate. Roll out top crust.

In large bowl combine first amount of sugar, flour and cinnamon. Stir.

Add apples and raisins. Stir together. Turn into pie shell.

Pour cream over top. Dampen edges and cover with top crust. Trim and crimp edges. Cut slits in top.

Sprinkle with remaining sugar. Bake on bottom shelf of 350°F (180°C) oven about 45 to 55 minutes until browned and apples are tender. Yield: 1 pie.

PLUM CREAM PIE

A variation worth trying. Creamy good.

Whipping cream	**1 cup**	**250 mL**
Cornstarch	**¹/₄ cup**	**60 mL**
Water	**¹/₄ cup**	**60 mL**
Egg yolks, beaten	**2**	**2**
Granulated sugar	**²/₃ cup**	**150 mL**
Blue-purple prune plums, **cut up and pitted**	**2 cups**	**500 mL**
Pastry for a 2 crust pie, see page 140		
Granulated sugar	**¹/₄-¹/₂ tsp.**	**1-2 mL**

Heat cream in heavy saucepan until it boils.

Mix cornstarch and water. Stir into boiling cream until it thickens.

Combine egg yolks and first amount of sugar. Stir briskly as you add to thickened cream.

Add plums. Stir. Remove from heat. Cool to lukewarm.

Roll pastry and line 9 inch (22 cm) pie shell. Roll top crust. Pour filling into pie shell. Dampen edges. Top with second crust. Trim and crimp to seal. Cut slits in top.

Sprinkle with remaining sugar. Bake on bottom shelf in 350°F (180°C) oven about 60 minutes until fruit is cooked. Yield: 1 pie.

SOUR CHERRY PIE

What a picture when you see a wedge of this pie. The small round red cherries look so inviting.

Canned red sour pitted cherries	2 x 14 oz.	2 x 398 mL
Granulated sugar	1 cup	250 mL
All-purpose flour	2 tbsp.	30 mL
Reserved cherry juice	3/4 cup	175 mL
Lemon juice	2 tsp.	10 mL
Almond flavoring	1/8 tsp.	0.5 mL
Cinnamon	1/8 tsp.	0.5 mL
Red food coloring drops	3-4	3-4
Pastry for 2 crust pie, see page 140		
Granulated sugar	1/4-1/2 tsp.	1-2 mL

Drain cherries. Measure and reserve 3/4 cup (175 mL) juice.

Measure first amount of sugar and flour into saucepan. Mix well. Add next 5 ingredients. Heat and stir until it boils and thickens. Remove from heat. Stir in cherries. Cool thoroughly.

Roll pastry and line 9 inch (22 cm) pie plate. Roll top crust. Pour cooled filling into pie shell. Dampen edges and apply top crust. Trim and crimp edges to seal. Cut vents in top.

Sprinkle with remaining sugar. Bake on bottom rack in 400°F (200°C) oven about 30 minutes until browned. Yield: 1 pie.

PLUM PIE

A plum juicy pie.

Pastry for a 2 crust pie, see page 140		
Blue-purple prune plums, sliced and pitted, about 1 1/2 lbs. (680 g)	4 cups	1 L
Minute tapioca	3 tbsp.	50 mL
Granulated sugar	1 cup	250 mL
Cinnamon	1/4 tsp.	1 mL
Lemon juice	2 tsp.	10 mL
Granulated sugar	1/4-1/2 tsp.	1-2 mL

(continued on next page)

Roll pastry and line 9 inch (22 cm) pie shell. Roll top crust.

In large bowl combine plums and tapioca. Stir well. Let stand 15 minutes.

Add first amount of sugar and cinnamon. Stir. Arrange in pie shell.

Sprinkle with lemon juice. Moisten edges of crust with water. Place second crust over top. Trim and crimp to seal. Cut slits in top.

Sprinkle with remaining sugar. Bake on bottom shelf of 350°F (180°C) oven about 60 minutes until fruit is cooked. Yield: 1 pie.

SOUR CREAM APPLE PIE

A rich one layer pie with a crumbly top. Really good.

Sour cream	1 cup	250 mL
Egg, fork beaten	1	1
Granulated sugar	3/4 cup	175 mL
All-purpose flour	1/4 cup	60 mL
Vanilla	1 tsp.	5 mL
Salt	1/4 tsp.	1 mL
Cooking apples, peeled, cored and sliced	4 cups	1 L
Unbaked 9 inch (22 cm) pie shell, see page 140	1	1
STREUSEL TOPPING		
All-purpose flour	2/3 cup	150 mL
Brown or white sugar	1/2 cup	125 mL
Butter or margarine	1/3 cup	75 mL
Cinnamon	1/2 tsp.	2 mL
Walnuts (optional)	1/2 cup	125 mL

Mix first 6 ingredients in bowl.

Add apples and stir.

Turn into pie shell.

Streusel Topping: Mix flour, sugar, butter and cinnamon until crumbly. Add walnuts. Stir and scatter over pie. Bake on bottom shelf in 375°F (190°C) oven about 50 minutes until browned and apples are tender. Rich enough to cut into 8 pieces. Yield: 1 pie.

RHUBARB PINEAPPLE PIE

A good combo. Rhubarb flavor is mild.

Granulated sugar	1¹/₄ cups	275 mL
All-purpose flour	¹/₄ cup	50 mL
Thinly sliced rhubarb	3 cups	700 mL
Crushed pineapple, drained	14 oz.	398 mL
Pastry for a 2 crust pie, see page 140		
Granulated sugar	¹/₄-¹/₂ tsp.	1-2 mL

In large bowl measure first amount of sugar and flour. Stir.

Add rhubarb and pineapple. Stir.

Roll pastry and line 9 inch (22 cm) pie plate. Roll top crust. Turn fruit mixture into pie shell. Moisten pastry rim. Cover with top crust. Trim and crimp to seal. Cut slits in top.

Sprinkle with remaining sugar. Bake on bottom shelf in 350° (180°C) oven about 50 to 60 minutes until browned and rhubarb is cooked. Yield: 1 pie.

1. Pineapple Glory Pie page 24
2. Maids of Honour page 146
3. Cocojam Tarts page 145
4. Fried Pies page 147
5. Chilled Cherry Pie page 44

RHUBARB CREAM PIE

Sort of custardy without any eggs in the filling.

Thinly sliced rhubarb	**4 cups**	**1 L**
Unbaked 9 inch (22 cm) pie shell, **see page 140**	**1**	**1**
Granulated sugar	**1¼ cups**	**300 mL**
All-purpose flour	**½ cup**	**125 mL**
Salt	**¼ tsp.**	**1 mL**
Whipping cream	**¾ cup**	**175 mL**

Place rhubarb in pie shell.

In small bowl stir sugar and flour well. Add salt and cream. Stir. Pour over rhubarb. Bake on bottom shelf in 350°F (180°C) oven about 55 minutes until browned and rhubarb is cooked. Yield: 1 pie.

CRANAPPLE PIE

A full and colorful pie. Good combination.

Pastry for a 2 crust pie, see page 140

Cranberries, fresh or frozen	**2 cups**	**450 mL**
Granulated sugar	**1¾ cups**	**400 mL**
Minute tapioca	**⅓ cup**	**75 mL**
Water	**¼ cup**	**60 mL**
Grated orange rind (optional)	**2 tsp.**	**10 mL**
Cooking apples, peeled, cored **and sliced (McIntosh is good)**	**3 cups**	**700 mL**
Granulated sugar	**¼-½ tsp.**	**1-2 mL**

Roll pastry and line 9 inch (22 cm) pie plate. Roll top crust. Use top crust as is or cut into strips 1 inch (2.5 cm) wide for lattice top.

Combine next 5 ingredients in saucepan. Heat and stir until it boils. Remove from heat.

Stir in apple. Set saucepan in cold water in sink for 10 minutes. Stir occasionally. Turn into pie shell. Moisten edge of crust. Cover with top crust or strips. Trim and press to seal. Cut vents in top crust.

Sprinkle with remaining sugar. Bake on bottom shelf in 350°F (180°C) oven for about 55 minutes until fruit is tender. Yield: 1 pie.

Pictured on cover.

RHUBARB SOUR CREAM PIE

Bite into this pie and . . . perfect bliss!

Rhubarb, in 1 inch (2.5 cm) lengths	4 cups	900 mL
Unbaked 9 inch (22 cm) pie shell, see page 140	1	1
Granulated sugar	1¹/₂ cups	350 mL
All-purpose flour	¹/₃ cup	75 mL
Sour cream	1 cup	250 mL
TOPPING		
All-purpose flour	¹/₂ cup	125 mL
Brown sugar, packed	¹/₂ cup	125 mL
Butter or margarine, softened	¹/₄ cup	60 mL

Place rhubarb in pie shell.

Stir sugar and flour together in small bowl. Mix in sour cream. Pour over rhubarb.

Topping: Mix all 3 ingredients until crumbly. Sprinkle over pie. Bake on bottom shelf in 425°F (220°C) oven for 10 minutes. Reduce heat to 350°F (180°C) and bake about 40 to 50 minutes until rhubarb is cooked and topping is browned. Yield: 1 pie.

RHUBARB FLUFF PIE

And light and airy fluff it is!

Water	¹/₃ cup	75 mL
Granulated sugar	1¹/₄ cups	275 mL
Thinly sliced rhubarb	3¹/₂ cups	800 mL
Salt	¹/₄ tsp.	1 mL
Unflavored gelatin	1 x ¹/₄ oz.	1 x 7 g
Cold water	¹/₄ cup	60 mL
Drops of red food coloring, if needed		
Whipping cream (or 1 envelope topping)	1 cup	250 mL
Baked 9 inch (22 cm) pie shell, see page 140	1	1

(continued on next page)

Measure first 4 ingredients into saucepan. Bring to a boil. Simmer until rhubarb is cooked.

Sprinkle gelatin over cold water in small dish. Let stand 1 minute. Add to hot mixture. Stir to dissolve.

Add food coloring to tint pink. Chill until quite syrupy. Stir occasionally as it thickens.

Beat cream in small bowl until stiff. Fold into chilled mixture.

Pour into pie shell. Chill. Yield: 1 pie.

RHUBARB CUSTARD PIE

Oh for a fresh juicy rhubarb pie like this one! A good take-along dessert.

Pastry for a 2 crust pie, see page 140		
Egg yolks	2	2
Granulated sugar	1 cup	250 mL
All-purpose flour	2 tbsp.	30 mL
Butter or margarine, melted	1 tbsp.	15 mL
Rhubarb, fresh or frozen, in 1/2 inch (12 mm) pieces	2 1/2 cups	600 mL
Granulated sugar	1/4-1/2 tsp.	1-2 mL

Roll pastry and fit into 9 inch (22 cm) pie shell. Roll pastry for top crust.

In small bowl beat egg yolks until thick and light colored. Transfer to larger bowl.

Add next 4 ingredients. Stir to mix. Pour into pie shell. Dampen edges. Top with second crust. Trim and crimp edge to seal. Cut vents in top.

Sprinkle with remaining sugar. Bake on bottom shelf in 450°F (230°F) oven for 10 minutes. Reduce heat to 325°F (160°C) oven and bake about 25 minutes until rhubarb is tender. Yield: 1 pie.

STRAWBERRY PIE

Just a delicious double crust red pie. If you usually have fresh glazed berries in a pie this will be a change you won't want to miss.

Pastry for a 2 crust pie, see page 140

Fresh strawberries, halved, quartered if large	**1 qt.**	**1 L**
Granulated sugar	**1 cup**	**250 mL**
Minute tapioca	**3 tbsp.**	**50 mL**
Granulated sugar	**$^1/_4$-$^1/_2$ tsp.**	**1-2 mL**
Whipped Cream, page 30 (optional)		

Roll pastry and line 9 inch (22 cm) pie plate. Roll top crust.

In large bowl place strawberries, first amount of sugar and minute tapioca. Mix. Let stand 15 minutes. Stir. Pour into pie shell. Dampen edge of pastry. Cover with top crust. Trim and crimp to seal. Cut vents in top.

Sprinkle with remaining sugar. Bake on bottom shelf in 350°F (180°C) oven about 45 minutes until cooked.

Serve with whipped cream. Yield: 1 pie.

PLUM CRUMB PIE

Great color to this brown-sugar-topped pie.

FILLING

Plums, cut up and pitted (peeled, optional)	**4 cups**	**1 L**
All-purpose flour	**$^1/_3$ cup**	**75 mL**
Granulated sugar	**1 cup**	**225 mL**
Cinnamon	**$^1/_2$ tsp.**	**2 mL**
Unbaked 9 inch (22 cm) pie shell, see page 140	**1**	**1**

TOPPING

All-purpose flour	**$^3/_4$ cup**	**175 mL**
Brown sugar, packed	**$^1/_2$ cup**	**125 mL**
Butter or margarine	**6 tbsp.**	**100 mL**

(continued on next page)

Filling: In large bowl mix plums, flour, sugar and cinnamon.

Turn into pie shell.

Topping: Measure flour and sugar into bowl. Cut in butter until crumbly. Spread over pie. Bake on bottom shelf in 350°F (180°C) oven about 45 minutes until browned and fruit is cooked. Yield: 1 pie.

RAISIN CREAM PIE

Raisins are well suspended in the cream filling and covered with meringue.

Raisins	1 cup	250 mL
Boiling Water	1 cup	250 mL
Granulated sugar	$^3/_4$ cup	175 mL
All-purpose flour	$^1/_4$ cup	50 mL
Egg yolks	3	3
Vanilla	1 tsp.	5 mL
Salt	$^1/_4$ tsp.	1 mL
Cream or rich milk	1 cup	250 mL
Baked 9 inch (22 cm) pie shell, see page 140	1	1
MERINGUE		
Egg whites (room temperature)	3	3
Cream of tartar	$^1/_4$ tsp.	1 mL
Granulated sugar	6 tbsp.	100 mL

Cook raisins in boiling water in covered saucepan for 10 minutes.

Stir sugar and flour together until thoroughly mixed. Mix in egg yolks, vanilla, salt and cream. Stir into boiling raisins until it boils and thickens. Remove from heat.

Pour into pie shell.

Meringue: Beat egg whites and cream of tartar in bowl until a stiff froth. Beat in sugar gradually, beating until stiff and sugar is dissolved. Spoon onto pie sealing around edge. Bake in 350°F (180°C) oven about 10 minutes until golden. Yield: 1 pie.

FRESH APRICOT PIE

There is nothing quite like a fresh fruit pie such as this.

Pastry for a 2 crust pie, see page 140

Granulated sugar	1 cup	250 mL
All-purpose flour	1/4 cup	60 mL
Nutmeg	1/8 tsp.	0.5 mL
Fresh apricots, quartered and pitted	4 cups	1 L
Prepared orange juice	1 tbsp.	15 mL
Lemon juice	2 tsp.	10 mL
Granulated sugar	1/4-1/2 tsp.	1-2 mL

Roll pastry and line 9 inch (22 cm) pie shell. Roll top crust.

In large bowl measure first amount of sugar, flour and nutmeg. Mix well. Add apricots. Stir together and pour into pie shell.

Combine orange and lemon juice. Drizzle over all. Dampen edge of crust. Place second crust over top. Trim and crimp to seal. Cut vents in top.

Sprinkle with remaining sugar. Bake on bottom shelf in 350°F (180°C) oven about 45 minutes until cooked and browned. Yield: 1 pie.

PEAR PIE

Fresh pears between two crusts make a perfect harvest pie. Quite uncommon. If you have never made one you will want to try it.

Granulated sugar	1/2 cup	125 mL
All-purpose flour	2 tbsp.	30 mL
Ginger	1/4 tsp.	1 mL
Cinnamon	1/8 tsp.	0.5 mL
Medium pears, peeled and sliced (Bartlett is best)	6-8	6-8

Pastry for a 2 crust pie, see page 140

Lemon juice	1 1/2 tbsp.	25 mL
Granulated sugar	1/4-1/2 tsp.	1-2 mL

(continued on next page)

Measure first 4 ingredients into large bowl. Stir.

Add pears and toss.

Roll pastry and line 9 inch (22 cm) pie plate. Roll top crust. Pour pear mixture into pie shell.

Drizzle lemon juice over top. Dampen crust edges. Lay top crust over. Trim and crimp to seal. Cut slits in top.

Sprinkle with remaining sugar. Bake on bottom shelf in 350°F (180°C) oven for about 60 minutes until browned and pears are cooked. Yield: 1 pie.

WINTER PIE

This resembles a mincemeat pie. Serve it warm with ice cream for a meal or perhaps for a coffee party.

Granulated sugar	1/2 cup	125 mL
Cornstarch	1 tbsp.	15 mL
Cinnamon	1/2 tsp.	3 mL
Cloves	1/4 tsp.	1 mL
Nutmeg	1/4 tsp.	1 mL
Salt	1/4 tsp.	1 mL
Seedless raisins	1 cup	250 mL
Finely chopped carrot	1/2 cup	125 mL
Hot water	1/2 cup	125 mL
Peeled and coarsely chopped apples	1 cup	250 mL
Pastry for a 2 crust pie, see page 140		
Granulated sugar	1/4 -1/2 tsp.	1-2 mL

In medium size saucepan measure first 6 ingredients. Stir well.

Add raisins and carrot. Stir in water. Stir over medium heat until boiling. Simmer 5 minutes. Remove from heat.

Add apples. Stir.

Roll pastry to fit 9 inch (22 cm) pie plate. Spoon in filling. Dampen outside edge. Top with more pastry. Trim and crimp edges. Cut slits in top.

Sprinkle with remaining sugar. Bake in 350°F (180°C) oven for about 40 to 45 minutes or until browned. Yield: 1 pie.

PINEAPPLE CHEESE PIE

Incredibly good. A must-try.

Crushed pineapple with juice	14 oz.	398 mL
Granulated sugar	²/₃ cup	150 mL
Cornstarch	2 tbsp.	30 mL
Cream cheese, softened	8 oz.	250 g
Granulated sugar	¹/₂ cup	125 mL
Eggs	2	2
Vanilla	³/₄ tsp.	4 mL
Salt	¹/₄ tsp.	1 mL
Milk	¹/₃ cup	75 mL
Unbaked 10 inch (25 cm) pie shell, see page 140	1	1
Whipped Cream, see page 30	1 cup	250 mL
Chopped macadamia nuts (or other)		

Combine first 3 ingredients in saucepan. Mix well until cornstarch is dissolved. Stir over medium heat until it boils 1 minute and is thickened. Cool.

In mixing bowl beat cream cheese and second amount of sugar. Beat in eggs 1 at a time until smooth. Mix in vanilla, salt and milk.

Spread pineapple mixture in pie shell. Pour cream cheese mixture over top. Bake on bottom shelf in 350°F (180°C) oven about 55 minutes until set. Cool.

Cover with whipped cream. Sprinkle with macadamia nuts. Yield: 1 pie.

When she heard there was a fork in the road she decided to go back to avoid a puncture.

GRATED APPLE PIE

A very different looking apple pie. Contains eggs, giving it a bit of a custardy effect. Good flavor. A single crust which allows shreds of apple to show.

Eggs	2	2
Granulated sugar	1 cup	250 mL
All-purpose flour	1 tbsp.	15 mL
Grated peeled apples (use medium grater) packed	2 cups	500 mL
Cinnamon	1/2 tsp.	2 mL
Unbaked 9 inch (22 cm) pie shell, see page 140	1	1

Beat eggs in medium size bowl until frothy. Beat in sugar and flour.

Add apple and cinnamon. Stir.

Turn into pie shell. Bake in 350°F (180°C) oven about 45 minutes until set and apple is cooked. Yield: 1 pie.

SNOW PIE

So light and so good. Like new fallen snow. Best eaten the same day. Very easy. Pie shell is baked twice.

Egg whites, room temperature	2	2
Granulated sugar	1 cup	250 mL
Grated peeled apple	1 cup	250 mL
Baked 9 inch (22 cm) pie shell, see page 140	1	1
Ice cream (optional)		

Beat egg whites in mixing bowl until a firm froth.

Gradually beat in sugar and apple until stiff.

Turn into baked pie shell. Bake in 350°F (180°C) oven for 15 to 20 minutes until set. Cool.

Top with ice cream. Yield: 1 pie.

APPLE PIE

This is the best pie if you want to indulge or if you need solace for contentment. The aroma that fills the air is heavenly. Serve with cheese and/or ice cream.

Pastry for a 2 crust pie, see page 140

Granulated sugar	**1 cup**	**250 mL**
All-purpose flour	**2 tbsp.**	**30 mL**
Cinnamon	**¹/₂ tsp.**	**2 mL**
Cooking apples, peeled, cored and cut up (McIntosh is good)	**5 cups**	**1.13 L**
Lemon juice	**2 tsp.**	**10 mL**
Granulated sugar	**¹/₄-¹/₂ tsp.**	**1-2 mL**

Roll pastry and fit into 9 inch (22 cm) pie plate. Roll out top crust.

In large bowl combine first amount of sugar, flour and cinnamon.

Add apple and stir. Turn into pie shell.

Sprinkle with lemon juice. Dampen edges and place second crust on top. Trim and crimp to seal. Cut slits in top.

Sprinkle with remaining sugar. Bake on bottom shelf in 350°F (180°C) oven for about 45 minutes until browned and apples are tender. Yield: 1 pie.

Note: Granulated sugar may be substituted with half brown sugar or all brown sugar in the filling.

RHUBARB PIE

An ordinary pie with a not so ordinary taste.

Pastry for a 2 crust pie, see page 140

Minute tapioca	**3 tbsp.**	**50 mL**
Rhubarb, cut in 1 inch (2.5 cm) lengths (red is best)	**4 cups**	**1 L**
Granulated sugar	**1¹/₂ cups**	**375 mL**
Salt	**¹/₈ tsp.**	**0.5 mL**
Granulated sugar for topping	**¹/₄-¹/₂ tsp.**	**1-2 mL**

(continued on next page)

Roll pastry and line 9 inch (22 cm) pie plate.

Combine tapioca, rhubarb, first amount of sugar and salt in large bowl. Toss. Let stand 15 minutes. Stir and turn into pie shell.

Roll pastry for top crust. Dampen edges, place crust on top. Trim and crimp to seal. Cut vents in top.

Sprinkle with remaining sugar. Bake on bottom shelf in 350°F (180°C) oven until cooked and browned about 45 to 55 minutes. Yield: 1 pie.

UPSIDE DOWN APPLE PIE

Sounds like it shouldn't work but it does. What a gorgeous plateful to present to guests with glistening pecans on top. They were the bottom layer at first.

Pecan or walnut halves	$^1/_2$ cup	125 mL
Brown sugar, packed	$^1/_3$ cup	75 mL
Granulated sugar	1 cup	250 mL
All-purpose flour	2 tbsp.	30 mL
Cinnamon	$^1/_2$ tsp.	2 mL
Salt	$^1/_8$ tsp.	0.5 mL
Lemon juice	2 tsp.	10 mL
Cooking apples, peeled, cored and sliced (McIntosh is good)	5 cups	1.13 L

Pastry for a 1 crust pie, see page 140

Line a 9 inch (22 cm) pie plate with a wide circle of foil. Take 2 pieces of 12 inch (30 cm) foil about 2 feet (60 cm) long. Make a drugstore fold lengthwise resulting in 1 large square. Press into pie plate. Grease foil heavily on bottom and sides up to top edge of pie plate. Place pecans or walnut halves round side down on bottom of foil in pie plate. Sprinkle with brown sugar.

Combine next 5 ingredients in large bowl. Stir well.

Add apples to dry mixture. Stir together. Spread over nuts in pie plate.

Roll pastry and place over top. Fold edges under and flute. Turn up foil all around. Trim foil if you like but leave it at least 4 inches (10 cm) high. Cut slits in pastry. Bake in 350°F (180°C) oven about 45 to 55 minutes until apples are cooked. Cover with large plate and invert so pie is upside down. Remove foil carefully. Serve warm. Yield: 1 pie.

Pictured on page 53.

CRANBERRY PIE

A favorite family pie for New Year's day. Whipped cream topping is a must.

Granulated sugar	³/₄ cup	175 mL
All-purpose flour	1¹/₂ tbsp.	25 mL
Boiling water	¹/₂ cup	125 mL
Salt	¹/₄ tsp.	1 mL
Cranberries, fresh or frozen	1¹/₂ cups	375 mL
Raisins	1 cup	250 mL
Unbaked 9 inch (22 cm) pie shell, see page 140	1	1
WHIPPED CREAM		
Whipping cream	1 cup	250 mL
Granulated sugar	2 tsp.	10 mL
Vanilla	¹/₂ tsp.	2 mL

Stir sugar and flour together. Add water and salt. Mix.

Grind cranberries and raisins. Add to sugar and flour mixture. Stir. If you have a food processor all ingredients can be put in and ground and mixed at the same time.

Pour filling into pie shell. Bake in 400°F (200°C) oven about 20 minutes until set. Cool.

Whipped Cream: Beat cream, sugar and vanilla in small bowl until thick. Spoon over pie. Chill. Yield: 1 pie.

Pictured on page 125.

MOCK CHERRY PIE: Coarsely chop cranberries and raisins rather than grind. Add ¹/₄ cup (50 mL) more sugar. Add almond flavoring to taste about ¹/₄ to ¹/₂ tsp (1 to 2 mL). Use 2 crusts. Bake until browned.

Paré Pointer

If you have a sick horse and a dead bee you have a seedy beast and a bee deceased.

An autumn pie with a choice of crumb toppings. A delectable taste.

Granulated sugar	1/4 cup	60 mL
All-purpose flour	1/4 cup	60 mL
Ginger	1/4 tsp.	1 mL
Medium pears, peeled and sliced (Bartlett is best)	7	7
Unbaked 9 inch (22 cm) pie shell, page 140	1	1
Corn syrup	1/4 cup	50 mL
Lemon juice	1 1/2 tbsp.	25 mL
STREUSEL TOPPING		
All-purpose flour	2/3 cup	150 mL
Brown sugar, packed	1/2 cup	125 mL
Butter or margarine	1/3 cup	75 mL

Stir first 3 ingredients together in large bowl.

Add pears. Stir.

Pour into pie shell.

Mix corn syrup and lemon juice. Drizzle over top.

Streusel Topping: Combine flour, sugar and butter. Mix until crumbly. Sprinkle over pie. Bake on bottom shelf in 350°F (180°C) oven about 60 to 70 minutes until browned and pears are cooked. Yield: 1 pie.

CRUMB TOPPING		
All-purpose flour	1/2 cup	125 mL
Granulated sugar, packed	1/2 cup	125 mL
Butter or margarine	1/3 cup	75 mL

Mix all 3 ingredients until crumbly.

Use this instead of Streusel Topping. Bake as directed. Makes a golden white topping rather than brown.

The ocean had nothing to say to the sandy beach, but it would wave often.

APPLE CREAM PIE

The addition of heavy cream gives this pie a richer juice.

Pastry for a 2 crust pie, see page 140

Granulated sugar	1 cup	250 mL
All-purpose flour	1/4 cup	60 mL
Cinnamon	1/2 tsp.	2 mL
Salt	1/8 tsp.	0.5 mL
Cooking apples, peeled, cored and cut up	5 cups	1.13 L
Whipping cream	1/2 cup	125 mL
Pastry strips, 1 inch (2.5 cm) wide for lattice crust (or leave as whole crust)		

Roll pastry and line a 9 inch (22 cm) pie plate.

Measure sugar, flour, cinnamon and salt into large bowl. Stir well.

Add apples to sugar mixture. Toss. Pour into pie shell.

Pour cream over top.

Dampen edges. Make lattice top on pie by placing pastry strips at right angles. Crimp ends to seal. Bake on bottom shelf in 375°F (190°C) oven about 45 minutes until apples are tender. Yield: 1 pie.

SOUR CREAM PEACH PIE

A two crust pie containing a sour cream custard filling along with fresh peaches.

Pastry for a 2 crust pie, see page 140

Sour cream	1 cup	250 mL
Brown sugar, packed	1 cup	250 mL
All-purpose flour	1/3 cup	75 mL
Egg, fork beaten	1	1
Cinnamon	1/4 tsp.	1 mL
Peeled and sliced peaches	2 1/2 cups	575 mL
Granulated sugar	1/4-1/2 tsp.	1-2 mL

(continued on next page)

Roll pastry and line 9 inch (22 cm) pie plate. Roll top crust. Cover with plastic wrap.

Combine next 5 ingredients in small bowl. Stir.

Immerse peaches in boiling water for 1 minute. Transfer to cold water. Peel and slice. Place peaches in pie shell. Pour sour cream mixture over top. Dampen edges of crust with water. Cover with top crust. Trim and crimp to seal. Cut vents in top.

Sprinkle with granulated sugar. Bake on bottom shelf in 425°F (220°C) oven for 10 minutes. Reduce heat to 350°F (180°C) and bake about 40 minutes until browned and peaches are cooked. Yield: 1 pie.

STRAWBERRY PINEAPPLE PIE

Pretty pink color. These flavors combine really well.

Granulated sugar	1 cup	250 mL
Cornstarch	2 tbsp.	30 mL
Fresh sliced strawberries	3 cups	700 mL
Crushed pineapple, drained	19 oz.	540 mL
Pastry for a 2 crust pie, see page 140		
Granulated sugar	$^1/_4$ -$^1/_2$ tsp.	1-2 mL

In large bowl mix first amount of sugar and cornstarch. Add strawberries and pineapple. Stir.

Roll pastry and line 9 inch (22 cm) pie plate. Roll top crust. Pour fruit mixture into pie shell. Moisten rim of crust. Top with pastry. Trim and crimp to seal. Cut slits in top.

Sprinkle with remaining sugar. Bake on bottom shelf in 350°F (180°C) oven about 50 minutes until browned and strawberries are cooked. Yield: 1 pie.

Paré Pointer

That skeleton running around is just a bunch of bones with the person off.

STRAWBERRY RHUBARB PIE

These two fruits complement each other.

Egg	1	1
All-purpose flour	3 tbsp.	50 mL
Granulated sugar	1 cup	250 mL
Rhubarb, cut in short pieces	3 cups	700 mL
Fresh sliced strawberries	1 cup	250 mL
Pastry for a 2 crust pie, see page 140		
Granulated sugar	$1/4 - 1/2$ tsp.	1-2 mL

Beat egg in large bowl. Mix in flour. Add first amount of sugar. Stir well.

Add rhubarb and strawberries. Stir.

Roll pastry. Line 9 inch (22 cm) pie plate. Roll top crust. Turn fruit mixture into pie shell. Moisten pastry rim. Place crust over top. Trim and crimp to seal. Cut slits in top.

Sprinkle with remaining sugar. Bake on bottom shelf in 350°F (180°C) oven about 45 minutes until browned and fruit is cooked. Yield: 1 pie.

1. Millionaire Pie page 41
2. Lemon Cheese Tarts page 79
3. Butter Tarts page 150
4. Sour Cream Tarts page 62
5. Cranberry Pie page 120
6. Banana Cream Pie page 74

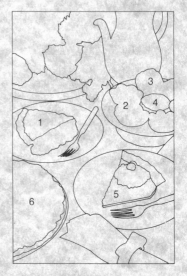

A mixture of four fruits in this colorful pie. Whipped cream or ice cream goes well with this.

**Pastry for a 2 crust pie,
   see page 140**

Granulated sugar	1¹/₃ **cups**	**300 mL**
All-purpose flour	¹/₃ **cup**	**75 mL**
Peeled and sliced cooking apples	**2 cups**	**450 mL**
Raspberries	**1 cup**	**250 mL**
Blackberries	**1 cup**	**250 mL**
Rhubarb, in short lengths	**1 cup**	**250 mL**
Granulated sugar	¹/₄-¹/₂ **tsp.**	**1-2 mL**

Roll pastry and line 9 inch (22 cm) pie plate. Roll top crust.

Stir first amount of sugar and flour together in large bowl.

Add apples, raspberries, blackberries and rhubarb. Toss well. Turn into pie shell. Dampen crust edge. Cover with pastry. Trim and crimp to seal. Cut vents in top.

Sprinkle with remaining sugar. Bake on bottom rack of 350°F (180°C) oven about 45 minutes until brown and apple is cooked. Yield: 1 pie.

A young child defines love, "I like Mom and Dad, but I love bubble gum".

ANGEL PIE

Graham cracker crumbs are added to this meringue crust. Whipped cream and grated chocolate are the crowning glory.

MERINGUE CRUST

Egg whites, room temperature	3	3
Cream of tartar	1/4 tsp.	1 mL
Granulated sugar	1 cup	225 mL
Vanilla	1 tsp.	5 mL
Baking powder	1 tsp.	5 mL
Graham cracker crumbs	1 cup	225 mL
Chopped pecans (or walnuts)	1 cup	225 mL
FILLING		
Whipping cream (or 1 envelope topping)	1 cup	250 mL
Granulated sugar	2 tsp.	10 mL
Vanilla	1/2 tsp.	2 mL
Grated semisweet chocolate	1/4 cup	50 mL
Grated semisweet chocolate	1-2 tbsp.	15-30 mL

Meringue Crust: Beat egg whites until foamy. Add cream of tartar and beat until soft peaks form. Add sugar gradually while continuing to beat until very stiff and all sugar is added.

Mix in vanilla and baking powder. Fold in graham crumbs and pecans. Spread over bottom and sides of greased 9 inch (22 cm) pie plate. Bake in 325°F (160°C) oven for 25 to 30 minutes. Cool on rack.

Filling: Beat cream, sugar and vanilla in small bowl until stiff.

Fold in first amount of grated chocolate. Spread over meringue crust.

Sprinkle with remaining grated chocolate. Chill. Yield: 1 pie.

CHOCOLATE ANGEL PIE

This will supply a chocolate fix for eight people.

Meringue Crust, see recipe above	1	1

(continued on next page)

FILLING

Semisweet chocolate chips	1 cup	250 mL
Water	3 tbsp.	50 mL
Instant coffee granules	½ tsp.	2 mL
Vanilla	1 tsp.	5 mL
Whipping cream (or 1 envelope topping)	1 cup	250 mL

Filling: In medium saucepan melt chocolate chips, water, coffee granules and vanilla. Stir often to hasten melting. Set saucepan in cold water to cool.

Beat cream in small bowl until thick. Fold into cooled chocolate mixture. Pour into shell. Chill several hours or overnight. Yield: 1 pie.

LEMON ANGEL PIE

Good lemon flavor in a chewy meringue crust.

Meringue Crust, see page 131	1	1
FILLING		
Egg yolks	3	3
Granulated sugar	½ cup	125 mL
Lemon juice	3 tbsp.	50 mL
Grated lemon rind	2 tsp.	10 mL
Whipping cream (or 1 envelope topping)	1 cup	250 mL

Prepare and bake Meringue Crust. Cool.

Filling: In top of double boiler or small heavy saucepan combine first 4 ingredients. Heat and stir until it boils and thickens. Remove from heat and cool.

Beat cream in small bowl until thick. Fold into cooled lemon mixture. Spread in meringue shell. Chill several hours before serving. Yield: 1 pie.

If your goat swallows your roll of film just hope nothing develops.

BROWNIE ANGEL PIE

The best two-tone for color and flavor. Chocolate cream is spread over a chewy chocolate base.

MERINGUE CRUST		
Egg whites, room temperature	3	3
Salt, just a pinch		
Cream of tartar	¹/₄ tsp.	1 mL
Granulated sugar	³/₄ cup	175 mL
Chocolate wafer crumbs	³/₄ cup	175 mL
Chopped pecans or walnuts	¹/₂ cup	125 mL
Vanilla	¹/₂ tsp.	2 mL
FILLING		
Whipping cream (or 1 envelope topping)	1 cup	250 mL
Cocoa (optional)	2 tbsp.	30 mL
Granulated sugar	1 tbsp.	15 mL
Vanilla	¹/₂ tsp.	2 mL
Grated chocolate	1-2 tbsp.	15-30 mL

Meringue Crust: Beat egg whites, salt and cream of tartar in mixing bowl until a stiff froth. Beat in sugar gradually, beating until very stiff and sugar is dissolved.

Fold in wafer crumbs, pecans and vanilla. Spread in greased 9 inch (22 cm) pie plate forming shell. Bake in 325°F (160°C) oven about 35 minutes until dry. Cool.

Filling: Beat cream, cocoa, sugar and vanilla in small bowl until stiff. Spread over pie.

Sprinkle with grated chocolate. Yield: 1 pie.

Pictured on page 71.

Paré Pointer

A net is really a bunch of holes tied together with string.

An absolute must. A real flavor-burst in this chewy pie.

MERINGUE CRUST

Egg whites, room temperature	3	3
Granulated sugar	1 cup	225 mL
Vanilla	1 tsp.	5 mL
Cracker crumbs (Ritz is good)	1 cup	225 mL
Chopped pecans (or walnuts)	³/₄ cup	175 mL

FILLING

Frozen raspberries in heavy syrup, (or strawberries) thawed	10 oz.	284 g

WHIPPED CREAM

Whipping cream (or 1 envelope topping)	1 cup	250 mL
Granulated sugar	2 tsp.	10 mL
Vanilla	¹/₂ tsp.	2 mL

Meringue Crust: Beat egg whites in bowl until soft peaks form. Add sugar gradually about 1 tbsp. (15 mL) at a time continuing to beat until all is used and egg whites are very stiff. Mix in vanilla.

Fold in cracker crumbs and pecans. Gently spread in greased 9 inch (22 cm) pie plate, covering bottom and sides. Bake in 325°F (160°C) oven for 25 to 30 minutes. Cool on rack. May be frozen at this point.

Filling: Spread cooled crust with raspberries.

Whipped Cream: Beat cream, sugar and vanilla in small bowl until stiff. Spoon over raspberries. Let stand 2 to 3 hours before cutting. Yield: 1 pie.

Chickens use fowl language to communicate.

PECAN TRIX

If you can't eat pecans, this pie will be next best to the real thing. Contains oatmeal. Like pecan pie.

Eggs	2	2
Corn syrup	1 cup	250 mL
Granulated sugar	1 cup	250 mL
Butter or margarine, melted	1/4 cup	50 mL
Quick cooking rolled oats	1 cup	250 mL
Unbaked 9 inch (22 cm) pie shell, see page 140	1	1

Beat eggs in small mixing bowl until frothy. Beat in next 4 ingredients.

Pour into pie shell. Bake on bottom rack in 350°F (180°C) oven about 50 minutes until set.

EGGNOG PIE

Include this in your food for the festive season. Tastes like eggnog.

Granulated sugar	1/2 cup	125 mL
Cornstarch	2 tbsp.	30 mL
Unflavored gelatin	1 x 1/4 oz.	1 x 7 g
Salt	1/4 tsp.	1 mL
Milk	1 1/4 cups	275 mL
Egg yolks, lightly beaten	3	3
Vanilla	1 1/2 tsp.	7 mL
Rum flavoring	1/2 tsp.	2 mL
Almond flavoring	1/4 tsp.	1 mL
Nutmeg	1/4 tsp.	1 mL
Whipping cream (or 1 envelope topping)	1 cup	250 mL
Maraschino cherries, sliced (optional)	4-8	4-8
Baked 9 inch (22 cm) pie shell, see page 140	1	1

(continued on next page)

Combine first four ingredients in saucepan. Stir well.

Slowly mix in milk. Heat and stir until it boils and thickens.

Stir about 1/2 cup (125 mL) hot mixture into egg yolks. Pour back into saucepan while stirring until it returns to a boil. Remove from heat.

Add vanilla, rum and almond flavorings and nutmeg. Chill until quite syrupy.

Whip cream in small mixing bowl until stiff. Fold into chilled mixture.

Fold in cherry slices. Pour into pie shell. Chill. Yield: 1 pie.

ZUCCHINI PIE

Looks like apple, feels like apple and tastes like apple.

Peeled, chopped zucchini	**7 cups**	**1.6 L**
Water	**1/2 cup**	**125 mL**
Granulated sugar	**1 cup**	**250 mL**
Cornstarch	**2 tbsp.**	**30 mL**
Cinnamon	**1 1/2 tsp.**	**7 mL**
Salt	**1/4 tsp.**	**1 mL**
Lemon juice	**1/4 cup**	**50 mL**
Pastry for a 2 crust pie, see page 140		
Granulated sugar	**1/4 -1/2 tsp.**	**1-2 mL**

Place zucchini and water in large saucepan. If using frozen zucchini do not add water. Bring to a boil. Cook uncovered, stirring often, about 10 minutes until tender and most of the water is gone. Volume will reduce about half.

Mix first amount of sugar, cornstarch, cinnamon and salt in bowl. Stir into zucchini along with lemon juice. Cook and stir until thick. Remove from heat. Set pan in cold water to cool for 10 minutes.

Roll pastry and line 9 inch (22 cm) pie plate. Pour filling into pie shell. Roll pastry for top crust. Dampen edges of bottom crust and add top. Trim and crimp to seal. Cut vents in top.

Sprinkle with remaining sugar. Bake on bottom shelf in 375°F (190°C) oven about 55 minutes until browned. Yield: 1 pie.

MOCK PUMPKIN PIE

Tasting the surprise ingredient, turnip, you will find it hard to believe that you are not eating pumpkin pie.

Eggs	2	2
Brown sugar, packed	³/₄ cup	175 mL
Cooked mashed yellow turnip (rutabaga)	1¹/₄ cups	275 mL
Cinnamon	1 tsp.	5 mL
Nutmeg	¹/₂ tsp.	2 mL
Ginger	¹/₂ tsp.	2 mL
Cloves	¹/₈ tsp.	0.5 mL
Salt	¹/₂ tsp.	2 mL
Evaporated milk	1¹/₄ cups	275 mL
Unbaked 9 inch (22 cm) pie shell, see page 140	1	1
Whipped Cream, see page 30		

Beat eggs lightly in bowl. Add and mix next 8 ingredients in order given.

Pour into pie shell. Bake on bottom shelf in 450°F (230°C) oven for 10 minutes. Reduce heat to 325°F (160°C) and bake for about 40 to 50 minutes until an inserted knife comes out clean. Cool.

Put a dollop of whipped cream on each piece or smooth over entire pie before cutting. Yield: 1 pie.

MOCK APPLE PIE

Tasting is believing!

Pastry for a 2 crust pie, see page 140		
Ritz crackers or soda crackers, broken up	1 cup	250 mL
Cinnamon	1 tsp.	5 mL
Water	1¹/₂ cups	350 mL
Granulated sugar	1¹/₂ cups	350 mL
Cream of tartar	1¹/₂ tsp.	7 mL
Granulated sugar	¹/₄-¹/₂ tsp.	1-2 mL

(continued on next page)

Roll and line 9 inch (22 cm) pie plate with pastry. Break crackers into 4 or 5 pieces each and put into pie shell. Sprinkle with cinnamon.

Stir water, first amount of sugar and cream of tartar together in saucepan. Bring to a boil. Cool to lukewarm. Pour over crackers. Roll top crust. Dampen edges of bottom crust and cover with top crust. Trim and crimp edges to seal. Cut vents in top.

Sprinkle with remaining sugar. Bake on bottom shelf in 350°F (180°C) oven about 45 minutes until browned. Yield: 1 pie.

Pictured on page 53.

VINEGAR PIE

When grocery stores were far and fresh lemons were scarce, this pie was a good substitute. Tastes like lemon pie.

Vinegar	$^1/_3$ cup	75 mL
Granulated sugar	$^1/_2$ cup	125 mL
Water	$1^3/_4$ cups	400 mL
Granulated sugar	$^1/_2$ cup	125 mL
All-purpose flour	6 tbsp.	100 mL
Egg yolks	3	3
Water	$^1/_4$ cup	50 mL
Lemon extract	1 tsp.	5 mL
Baked 9 inch (22 cm) pie shell, see page 140	1	1
MERINGUE		
Egg whites, room temperature	3	3
Vinegar	$^1/_2$ tsp.	2 mL
Granulated sugar	6 tbsp.	100 mL

Measure vinegar, first amounts of sugar and water into saucepan. Stir. Bring to a boil over medium heat.

In small bowl mix next 5 ingredients. Stir into boiling mixture until it returns to a boil and thickens.

Pour into pie shell.

Meringue: Beat egg whites and vinegar in small mixing bowl until a stiff froth. Add sugar gradually, beating until stiff and sugar is dissolved. Spread over pie, sealing well to crust all around. Bake in 350°F (180°C) oven about 10 minutes until browned. Yield: 1 pie.

SWEET POTATO PIE

Serve this with whipped cream and you will think you are enjoying pumpkin pie.

Eggs	2	2
Cooked, mashed sweet potato	1½ cups	350 mL
Brown sugar, packed	¾ cup	175 mL
Butter or margarine, softened	2 tbsp.	30 mL
Cinnamon	¾ tsp.	4 mL
Ginger	¾ tsp.	4 mL
Allspice	¼ tsp.	1 mL
Salt	½ tsp.	2 mL
Milk	1¼ cups	275 mL
Vanilla	1 tsp.	5 mL
Unbaked 9 inch (22 cm) pie shell, see page 140	1	1

Beat eggs in mixing bowl until frothy. Mix in next 7 ingredients in order given.

Slowly mix in milk and vanilla.

Pour into pie shell. Bake on bottom shelf in 350°F (180°C) oven about 60 to 70 minutes until a knife inserted near center comes out clean. Yield: 1 pie.

GREEN TOMATO PIE

Use your surplus green tomatoes for this pie. It resembles apple pie.

Pastry for a 2 crust pie, see page 140

Green tomatoes, thinly sliced	2 cups	500 mL
Granulated sugar	2 cups	500 mL
Minute tapioca	2 tbsp.	30 mL
Cinnamon	½ tsp.	2 mL
Nutmeg	⅛ tsp.	0.5 mL
Lemon juice	1½ tbsp.	25 mL
Granulated sugar	¼-½ tsp.	1-2 mL

(continued on next page)

Roll out pastry and line 9 inch (22 cm) pie plate. Roll top crust.

Combine next 6 ingredients in bowl. Stir well. Let stand 15 minutes. Turn into pie shell. Dampen edges of pastry. Cover with top crust. Trim and seal. Cut slits in top.

Sprinkle with remaining sugar. Bake in 375°F (190°C) oven for about 45 minutes until filling is soft when poked with a knife. Cool. Yield: 1 pie.

CARROT PIE

From the depression era. Tastes like pumpkin pie.

Eggs	2	2
Granulated sugar	$1/2$ cup	125 mL
Cinnamon	$3/4$ tsp.	4 mL
Nutmeg	$1/2$ tsp.	2 mL
Ginger	$1/2$ tsp.	2 mL
Cloves	$1/8$ tsp.	0.5 mL
Cooked mashed carrot	1 cup	250 mL
Milk	$1 1/2$ cups	350 mL
Molasses (optional but good)	1 tbsp.	15 mL
Unbaked 10 inch (25 cm) pie shell, see page 140	1	1
Whipped Cream, see page 30		

Beat eggs lightly in bowl. Add and mix in next 8 ingredients in order given.

Pour into pie shell. Bake on bottom shelf in 450°F (230°C) oven for 10 minutes. Lower heat to 350°F (180°C) oven and cook about 45 minutes until an inserted knife comes out clean. Cool.

Smooth whipped cream over pie. Yield: 1 pie.

Note: A 9 inch (22 cm) pie shell may be used. There will be about $2/3$ cup (150 mL) filling left over that will need to be cooked in a separate container.

GRAPENUT PIE

A satiny filling with a crusty top. Serve with whipped cream. Resembles pecan pie.

Grapenut cereal	¹/₂ cup	125 mL
Warm water	¹/₂ cup	125 mL
Eggs	3	3
Granulated sugar	³/₄ cup	175 mL
Dark corn syrup	1 cup	250 mL
Butter or margarine, melted	3 tbsp.	50 mL
Vanilla	1 tsp.	5 mL
Unbaked 9 inch (22 cm) pie shell, see page 140	1	1

Combine cereal and water in bowl. Let stand until needed.

Beat eggs in small mixing bowl until frothy. Beat in sugar, syrup, butter and vanilla. Stir in softened cereal.

Pour into pie shell. Bake on bottom shelf in 350°F (180°C) oven about 50 minutes until puffed and set. Yield: 1 pie.

PEANUT BUTTER CRUST

Excellent with a banana cream filling, a cream filling or a chocolate filling.

All-purpose flour	1 cup	225 mL
Granulated sugar	2 tsp.	10 mL
Baking powder	¹/₄ tsp.	1 mL
Salt	¹/₄ tsp.	1 mL
Butter or margarine	¹/₄ cup	50 mL
Smooth peanut butter	¹/₄ cup	50 mL
Water	2 tbsp.	30 mL

Combine first 6 ingredients in mixing bowl. Beat on low speed until crumbly.

Add water. Work into a ball. Roll on lightly floured surface. Line 9 inch (22 cm) pie plate. Flute edge. Prick all over with tines of fork. Bake in 400°F (200°C) oven for 8 to 10 minutes. Yield: 1 pie shell.

HOT WATER PASTRY

Easy to whip up, but must be chilled prior to using.

Lard or shortening, room temperature, cut up	1 lb.	454 g
Boiling water	1 cup	225 mL
All-purpose flour	6 cups	1.35 L
Baking powder	1 tsp.	5 mL
Salt	1 tsp.	5 mL

Place lard in mixing bowl. Add boiling water. Beat until it is consistency of whipped cream.

Add remaining ingredients. Stir and mix until blended. Divide into 4 large patty-shaped balls. Wrap. Chill overnight. Makes 3 to 4 double crust pies.

MARGARINE PASTRY

Use low cholesterol margarine.

Cold margarine (not whipped)	1 lb.	454 g
All-purpose flour	5 cups	1.13 L
Salt	½ tsp.	2 mL
Baking powder	1 tsp.	5 mL
Cold water	½ cup	125 mL

Cut margarine into flour, salt and baking powder in mixing bowl until mixture is crumbly.

Sprinkle water over top. Mix with fork and press into large ball. Add a bit more water if needed, 1 to 2 tbsp. (15 to 30 mL). Divide into 4 parts. Shape into 4 patties. Roll for pie shells. Yield: 7 to 8 pie shells.

Paré Pointer

Said the beaver to the tree, "It's been nice gnawing you".

FAVORITE PIE CRUST

The pick of the lot.

All-purpose flour	5 cups	1.13 L
Brown sugar	3 tbsp.	50 mL
Salt	2 tsp.	10 mL
Baking powder	1 tsp.	5 mL
Lard, fairly cold	1 lb.	454 g
Egg	1	1
Vinegar	2 tbsp.	30 mL
Cold water to make	1 cup	225 mL

Measure flour, sugar, salt and baking powder into large bowl. Cut in lard until the size of tiny peas.

Break egg into measuring cup. Beat with fork. Add vinegar. Pour in enough water to measure 1 cup (225 mL). Pour a little at a time over flour mixture, tossing and stirring with fork until all liquid is absorbed. Shape into ball. Divide into 4 flattish balls. Wrap and refrigerate. Store in refrigerator up to 2 weeks. Freeze to have a continuing supply on hand. Yield: 6 to 8 shells.

BAKED PIE SHELL: A simple method to bake a pie shell is to cover the outside of an upside down pie plate. You don't get a fancy fluted edge, but you always have sides. Place another pie plate over almost cool crust, turn and release. It won't quite touch the bottom of second pie plate but you will never be able to tell once it is filled. Whether you bake pastry inside or outside of pie plate prick all over with fork before baking in 400°F (200°C) oven about 10 to 15 minutes until lightly browned. The most common size is 9 inch (22 cm). To have a fluted edge, line pan with pastry ½ inch (12 mm) wider than pan all around. Fold under and flute (crimp) with fingers.

TART SHELLS: Line 2 ⅝ inch (7 cm) muffin cups with pastry. Measure with string to determine diameter of circle needed. Other sizes may also be used from larger to smaller.

BAKED TART SHELLS: Measure outside measurement of muffin cup to determine diameter of circle needed. Cut out circles. Fit over outside of cups. Press 4 corners together. Prick all over with fork. Bake in 400°F (200°C) oven about 10 to 15 minutes until browned. Remove from pan while a bit warm. Shells may also be pricked and baked inside muffin cups but be prepared for shrinkage. Various sizes of tart molds may also be used.

PUFFY PASTRY

A nice soft dough. Easy to work with. Rich and actually puffy.

All-purpose flour	**1¹/₂ cups**	**375 mL**
Butter	**1 cup**	**250 mL**
Sour cream	**¹/₂ cup**	**125 mL**

Place flour and butter in bowl. Cut in butter until the size of small peas.

Add sour cream. Stir with fork until it holds together. Shape into 2 or 3 patty-shaped balls. Chill in plastic bag overnight. When ready to use, roll pastry quite thin. Yield: 1 pie shell.

BEST OIL PASTRY

Simple to make. Very tender.

Pastry flour (or all-purpose)	**1¹/₂ cups**	**375 mL**
Granulated sugar	**1 tsp.**	**5 mL**
Salt	**¹/₂ tsp.**	**2 mL**
Cooking oil	**¹/₂ cup**	**125 mL**
Milk	**2 tbsp.**	**30 mL**

Combine flour, sugar and salt in bowl. Stir.

Stir cooking oil and milk together well. Add to dry mixture. Mix until it forms a ball. Roll between 2 sheets of waxed paper or press into 9 inch (22 cm) pie plate. May be pricked with fork and baked or filled and baked. Yield: 1 pie shell.

Geometry teachers only eat square meals.

OLD TIME PASTRY

An ancient recipe still used today.

Shortening (or lard)	1 lb.	454 g
All-purpose flour	4 cups	900 mL
Baking powder (optional)	1 tsp.	5 mL
Salt (optional)	1 tsp.	5 mL
Cold water	¹/₂ cup	125 mL

Place first 4 ingredients in large bowl. Using table knife cut shortening into walnut size pieces. With pastry cutter, cut shortening in until the size of small peas.

Sprinkle water over top. Toss and stir with fork until it clings and you can form a ball. Divide into 4 flat patties. Wrap and chill. Yield: 6 shells.

DOUBLE CRUST: For a 9 inch (22 cm) pie use 1¹/₂ cups (375 mL) all-purpose flour, ³/₄ cup (150 mL) shortening and 6 tbsp. (100 mL) water.

ORANGE JUICE PASTRY: Use prepared orange juice instead of water.

1. Sugar Pie page 75
2. Butterscotch Pie page 61
3. Sour Cream Date Pie page 101

STRAWBERRY CHEESE TARTS

These are best served the same day they are made.

Semisweet chocolate chips, melted	1/2 cup	125 mL
Baked Tart Shells, see page 140	12	12
Cream cheese, softened	4 oz.	125 g
Granulated sugar	1/2 cup	125 mL
Sour cream	3 tbsp.	50 mL
Orange flavoring	1/4 tsp.	1 mL
Vanilla	1/4 tsp.	1 mL
TOPPING		
Fresh strawberries, sliced	24	24
Strawberry jelly preserves, melted	2 tbsp.	30 mL

Spoon about 1 tsp. (5 mL) chocolate in bottom of tart shells. Chill to set.

Beat cream cheese, sugar and sour cream together in small bowl until smooth. Mix in orange flavoring and vanilla. Spoon over chocolate. Chill for about 1 hour.

Topping: Arrange strawberries over filling. Use pastry brush to dab strawberry jelly over berries. Chill. Yield: 12 tarts.

COCOJAM TARTS

Red jam with a coconut topping. Very easy to eat.

Raspberry jam (or your favorite)	12 tsp.	60 mL
Unbaked Tart Shells, see page 140	12	12
Egg	1	1
Granulated sugar	3/4 cup	175 mL
Corn syrup	3 tbsp.	50 mL
Medium coconut	3/4 cup	175 mL
Vanilla	3/4 tsp.	4 mL
Salt	1/4 tsp.	1 mL

Put 1 tsp. (5 mL) jam in bottom of each tart shell.

Beat egg in small bowl until frothy. Beat in sugar and corn syrup. Stir in coconut, vanilla and salt. Cover jam with mixture, filling shells 2/3 full. Bake on bottom shelf in 400°F (200°C) oven about 10 minutes until pastry is browned. Yield: 12 to 14 tarts.

Pictured on page 107.

MAIDS OF HONOUR

Little jam-based tarts with a cakey filling.

Raspberry jam	12 tsp.	60 mL
Unbaked Tart Shells, see page 140	12	12
FILLING		
Butter or margarine, softened	1/4 cup	50 mL
Granulated sugar	1/4 cup	50 mL
Egg, beaten	1	1
All-purpose flour	1/2 cup	125 mL
Baking powder	1/4 tsp.	1 mL
Vanilla or almond flavoring	1/4 tsp.	1 mL
Icing (confectioner's) sugar		

Put small spoonful of jam in each tart shell.

Filling: Cream butter and sugar together well. Beat in egg.

Add flour, baking powder and vanilla. Stir to mix. Put about 1 tbsp. (15 mL) over jam in each tart shell. Bake on bottom shelf in 375°F (190°C) oven about 20 minutes until risen and firm. An inserted wooden pick should come out clean.

Dust with icing sugar to serve. Yield: 12 tarts.

Pictured on page 107.

JAM TARTS

We started making these in our family simply to use leftover pastry. They were so good, they ended up being made on purpose.

Raspberry jam
Apricot jam
Unbaked Tart Shells, see page 140

Place a large spoonful of raspberry jam in some tart shells and a spoonful of apricot jam in others. Bake on lower shelf in 400°F (200°C) oven until crust is browned. If you are baking a pie at the same time in a 350°F (180°C) oven, bake tarts at the same temperature but a little longer until pastry browns.

Pictured on page 89.

If you have never heard of these, you will want to make some soon. Different.

Canned apricots, drained	14 oz.	398 mL
Granulated sugar	1/2 cup	125 mL
Lemon juice (or to taste)	2 tsp.	10 mL
Cornstarch	2 tbsp.	30 mL

Pastry, see page 140

Fat for deep-frying

Icing (confectioner's) sugar

Mash apricots in medium saucepan. Add sugar, lemon juice and cornstarch. Stir well. Heat and stir until it boils and thickens. It will be thick.Cool thoroughly.

Roll pastry. Cut into sixteen 5 inch (13 cm) circles. Place pastry circle on saucer. Spoon 1 tbsp. (15 mL) fruit on half the circle. Dampen half the circle edge. Fold over and seal with fork.

Deep-fry in 400°F (200°C) hot fat about 3 minutes until browned on both sides. Drain on paper towels.

To serve, sift icing sugar over each pie. Yield: 16.

Pictured on page 107.

CHOCOLATE FRIED PIES

Milk	1/2 cup	125 mL
Granulated sugar	1/3 cup	75 mL
Cocoa	1 1/2 tbsp.	25 mL
All-purpose flour	1 1/2 tbsp.	25 mL
Egg	1	1
Vanilla	1/4 tsp.	1 mL

Heat milk and sugar in small saucepan, stirring often until it boils.

Meanwhile, mix cocoa and flour in small bowl. Add egg and vanilla. Mix well. Stir into boiling milk until it boils again and thickens. Makes about 6 fried pies.

MORE FRIED PIES: Try other fillings you like. Make only with cooked fillings.

APRICOT TARTS

Canned apricots end up in tart shells over a bit of custard. They look like fried eggs, sunny side up.

Granulated sugar	3 tbsp.	50 mL
All-purpose flour	3 tbsp.	50 mL
Milk	1 cup	250 mL
Vanilla	1 tsp.	5 mL
Baked Tart Shells, see page 140	12	12
Canned apricot halves, drained, juice reserved	14 oz.	398 mL
Reserved apricot juice	$1/2$ cup	125 mL
Lemon juice	$1/2$ tsp.	2 mL
Cornstarch	1 tbsp.	15 mL
Granulated sugar	2 tbsp.	30 mL
Lemon juice	1 tsp.	5 mL

In small saucepan mix first amount of sugar and flour well. Add milk and vanilla. Stir until smooth. Bring to a boil over medium heat, stirring until thickened. Remove from heat and cool slightly.

Spoon into tart shells.

Place 1 apricot half cut side down over cream filling in each tart shell.

Mix remaining ingredients in small saucepan. Stir as it comes to a boil and thickens. Cool a bit. Add lemon juice. Brush or spoon over apricots. Yield: 12 tarts.

As the vampire got out of the dentist's chair he said "Fangs so much".

CHOCOLATE TARTS

Intensely chocolate!

Semisweet baking chocolate squares, cut up	3 x 1 oz.	3 x 28 g
Egg yolks	3	3
Egg whites, room temperature	3	3
Whipping cream (or ³/₄ envelope topping)	³/₄ cup	175 mL
Rum flavoring	³/₄ tsp.	4 mL
Baked Tart Shells, see page 140	12	12

Melt chocolate in saucepan over low heat.

Add egg yolks. Beat until smooth and thick.

Using clean beaters, beat egg whites in small bowl until stiff. Set aside.

In another small bowl, using same beaters, beat cream until stiff. Mix in rum flavoring. Fold egg white into chocolate. Fold in whipped cream.

Spoon into tart shells. Chill. Yield: 12 tarts.

BUTTERSCOTCH TARTS

A rich tart. Contains butterscotch chips, coconut and walnuts.

Butter or margarine, softened	¹/₄ cup	60 mL
Brown sugar, packed	1 cup	250 mL
Egg	1	1
Vanilla	¹/₂ tsp.	2 mL
Chopped walnuts	2 tbsp.	30 mL
Medium coconut	2 tbsp.	30 mL
Butterscotch chips	1 cup	250 mL
Unbaked Tart Shells, see page 140	12	12

In mixing bowl cream butter and sugar together with spoon. Beat in egg and vanilla. Stir in walnuts, coconut and chips.

Spoon into tart shells, filling ²/₃ full. Bake in 375°F (190°C) oven about 15 to 20 minutes until golden brown. Yield: 12 tarts.

MINCE TARTS

A family favorite eaten warm, topped with ice cream. With a good supply in the freezer they may be enjoyed all year.

Mincemeat, run through blender	2 cups	450 mL
Applesauce	¾ cup	175 mL
Minute tapioca	1½ tbsp.	25 mL
Unbaked tart shells, see page 140	36	36
Pastry tops to fit tart shells	36	36
Granulated sugar	1 tsp.	5 mL

In small bowl mix mincemeat, applesauce and minute tapioca.

Spoon into tart shells about ¾ full. Dampen edge of pastry all around. Place top crust on. Press around edge to seal. Cut 2 to 3 small vents in top.

Sprinkle with a bit of sugar. Bake on bottom shelf in 400°F (200°C) oven about 15 minutes until browned. Filling will keep for months in the refrigerator. Makes about 2¾ cups (625 mL) or 36 tarts.

BUTTER TARTS

A great gooey, runny filling.

Raisins, coarsely chopped (or currants)	⅓ cup	75 mL
Pastry lined tart shells	12	12
Egg	1	1
Brown sugar, packed	½ cup	125 mL
Butter or margarine, softened	3 tbsp.	50 mL
Corn syrup	¼ cup	60 mL
Vinegar	1½ tsp.	7 mL
Vanilla	¼ tsp.	1 mL
Salt	⅛ tsp.	0.5 mL
Chopped walnuts (optional)		

Divide raisins among tart shells.

Beat egg with spoon in bowl until smooth. Mix in next 7 ingredients in order given. Spoon over raisins. Tart shells should be ⅔ full. Bake on bottom shelf in 375°F (190°C) oven for about 12 to 15 minutes until pastry is browned and filling rises up but doesn't break the surface. Cool. These freeze well. Yield: 12 tarts.

Pictured on page 125.

Throughout this book measurements are given in Imperial and Metric measure. To compensate for differences between the two measurements due to rounding, a full metric measure is not always used.

The cup used is the standard 8 fluid ounce. Temperature is given in degrees Fahrenheit and Celsius. Baking Pan measurements are in inches and centimetres as well as quarts and litres. An exact conversion is given below as well as the working equivalent (Standard Measure).

IMPERIAL	METRIC Exact Conversion	Standard Measure
Spoons	**millilitre (mL)**	**millilitre (mL)**
1/4 teaspoon (tsp.)	1.2 mL	1 mL
1/2 teaspoon (tsp.)	2.4 mL	2 mL
1 teaspoon (tsp.)	4.7 mL	5 mL
2 teaspoons (tsp.)	9.4 mL	10 mL
1 tablespoon (tbsp.)	14.2 mL	15 mL
Cups		
1/4 cup (4 tbsp.)	56.8 mL	50 mL
1/3 cup (5 1/3 tbsp.)	75.6 mL	75 mL
1/2 cup (8 tbsp.)	113.7 mL	125 mL
2/3 cup (10 2/3 tbsp.)	151.2 mL	150 mL
3/4 cup (12 tbsp.)	170.5 mL	175 mL
1 cup (16 tbsp.)	227.3 mL	250 mL
4 1/2 cups	1022.9 mL	1000 mL, 1 litre (1 L)
Ounces (oz.)	**Grams (g)**	**Grams (g)**
1 oz.	28.3 g	30 g
2 oz.	56.7 g	55 g
3 oz.	85.0 g	85 g
4 oz.	113.4 g	125 g
5 oz.	141.7 g	140 g
6 oz.	170.1 g	170 g
7 oz.	198.4 g	200 g
8 oz.	226.8 g	250 g
16 oz.	453.6 g	500 g
32 oz.	907.2 g	1000 g, 1 kilogram (1 kg)

PANS, CASSEROLES

Imperial	Metric	Imperial	Metric
8x8 inch	20x20 cm	1 2/3 qt.	2 L
9x9 inch	22x22 cm	2 qt.	2.5 L
9x13 inch	22x33 cm	3 1/3 qt.	4 L
10x15 inch	25x38 cm	1 qt.	1.2 L
11x17 inch	28x43 cm	1 1/4 qt.	1.5 L
8x2 inch round	20x5 cm	1 2/3 qt.	2 L
9x2 inch round	22x5 cm	2 qt.	2.5 L
10x4 1/2 inch tube	25x11 cm	4 1/4 qt.	5 L
8x4x3 inch loaf	20x10x7 cm	1 1/4 qt.	1.5 L
9x5x3 inch loaf	23x12x7 cm	1 2/3 qt.	2 L

OVEN TEMPERATURES

Fahrenheit (°F)	Celsius (°C)
175°	80°
200°	95°
225°	110°
250°	120°
275°	140°
300°	150°
325°	160°
350°	175°
375°	190°
400°	205°
425°	220°
450°	230°
475°	240°
500°	260°

INDEX

Angel Pie 128
Angel Pies, See Meringue Crust Pies
Apple Cream Pie 122
Apple Pie 118
Apple Pies
  Cranapple 109
  Crustless 57
  Deep 96
  Dutch 93
  Grated 117
  Snow 117
  Sour Cream 105
  Upside Down 119
Apple Raisin Pie 102
Apricot
  Fresh 114
  Fried Pies 147
Apricot Tarts 148

Baked Alaska Pie 84
Baked Pie Shell 140
Baked Tart Shells 140
Bakewell Tart 14
Banana Cream Pie 74
Berry Angel Pie 131
Best Oil Pastry 141
Black Bottom Lemon Pie 65
Black Bottom Pie 64
Blackberries
  Party Peach 97
Blueberry Alaska 84
Blueberry Pie 94
Blueberry Pies
  Chilled 21
  Glazed 50
Blueberry Sauce 77
Brandy Alexander Pie 25
Brownie Angel Pie 130
Brownie Pie 12
Bumbleberry Pie 127
Butter Tarts 150
Buttermilk Pie 70
Butterscotch Pie 61
Butterscotch Tarts 149

Cakey Pies or Tarts
  Bakewell 14
  Brownie 12
  French Coconut 19
  Lemon Chess 10
  Lemon Sponge 10
  Shoofly 8
Candy Pecan Pie 14
Canned Pear Pie 102
Caramel Pie 63
Caramel Sauce 78
Carrot Pie 137
Cheese Pie 43

Cherry No-Crust Pie 58
Cherry Pies
  Chilled 44
  Gelatin 51
  Glazed 19
  Pineapple Glory 24
  Sour 104
Cherry Pine Pie 47
Cherry Pineapple Pie 28
Chess Pie, Lemon 10
Chiffon Pies
  Brandy Alexander 25
  Chocolate Mocha 23
  Daiquiri 22
  Grapefruit 40
  Lemon 46
  Lime 22
  Orange 39
  Pineapple 45
  Pineapple Deluxe 29
  Pumpkin 27
  Rhubarb 38
  Sour Cream 55
  Watermelon 49
Chilled Blueberry Pie 21
Chilled Cherry Pie 44
Chilled Fruit Cocktail Pie 50
Chilled Maple Pie 33
Chilled Pies
  Cheese 43
  Cherry Pine 47
  Cherry Pineapple 28
  Chocolate Mint 46
  Chocolate Mocha 32
  Cocktail 37
  Coffee Toffee 26
  Creamy Lemon 52
  Creamy Lime 44
  Daiquiri 22
  French Silk 48
  Fresh Strawberry 40
  Gelatin Cherry 51
  Glazed Blueberry 50
  Glazed Cherry 19
  Grasshopper 42
  Key Lime 44
  Lemonade 37
  Light Strawberry 32
  Maple Pecan 30
  Millionaire 41
  Orange Mousse 38
  Peach Ice Cream 34
  Pineapple Glory 24
  Pineapple Wink 20
  Pink Velvet 42
  Raspberry Citrus 21
  Rhubarb Fluff Pie 110
  Strawberry Cheese 31
  Sweet Pineapple 56

Choco Mint Pie 82
Chocolate Angel Pie 128
Chocolate Coconut Pie 60
Chocolate Cookie Crust 29
Chocolate Crisp Crust 82
Chocolate Fried Pies 147
Chocolate Graham Crust 85
Chocolate Mint Pie 46
Chocolate Mocha Chiffon Pie 23
Chocolate Mocha Pie 32
Chocolate Pecan Pie 12
Chocolate Pie Shell 26
Chocolate Pies
    Brownie 12
    Brownie Angel 130
    Candy Pecan 14
    Choco Mint 82
    French Silk 48
    Frozen 83
    Mint 46
    No-Crust Fudge 58
Chocolate Pies, Partially
    Black Bottom 64
    Black Bottom Lemon 65
    Kentucky Derby 12
    Layered Fudge Frost 81
    Mud 86
    Pecan 12
    Strawberry Cheese 31
    Turtle 13
Chocolate Sauce 81
Chocolate Tarts 149
Cocktail Pie 37
Cocojam Tarts 145
Coconut Cream Pie 67
Coconut Meringue Pie 67
Coconut Pies
    Chocolate 60
    Coral Reef 100
    French 19
    Impossible 56
Coffee Toffee Pie 26
Coffee Topping 26
Concord Grape Pie 95
Coral Reef Pie 100
Cottage Cheese Pie 60
Cranapple Pie 109
Cranberry Pie 120
Cranberry Pies
    Cranapple 109
    Mock Cherry 120
Cream Pie 74
Cream Pies, See Custard And Cream
Creamy Lemon Pie 52
Creamy Lime Pie 44
Creamy Peanut Butter Pie 88
Crème de Menthe, See Grasshopper

Crumb Topping 121
Crustless Apple Pie 57
Crustless Pies
    Apple 57
    Cherry No-Crust 58
    Impossible 56
    Impossible Pumpkin 59
    No-Crust Fudge 58
Custard Pie 62
Custard Sauce 78
Custard And Cream Pies
    Banana 74
    Black Bottom 64
    Black Bottom Lemon 65
    Buttermilk 70
    Butterscotch 61
    Caramel 63
    Chocolate Coconut 60
    Coconut 67
    Coconut Meringue 67
    Cottage Cheese 60
    Flapper 73
    Lemon 77
    Lemon Meringue 65
    Lime Meringue 65
    Macadamia Nut 74
    Orange Meringue 69
    Peanut Butter 66
    Pumpkin 75
    Pumpkin Cheese 76
    Pumpkin Streusel 68
    Sour Cream 62
    Sugar 75

Daiquiri Pie 22
Date, Sour Cream Pie 101
Deep Apple Pie 96
Double Crust 142
Dutch Apple Pie 93

Eggnog Pie 132

Favorite Pie Crust 140
Filling
    Lemon Cheese 79
Flapper Pie 73
French Coconut Pie 19
French Silk Pie 48
Fresh Apricot Pie 114
Fresh Strawberry Pie 40
Fried Pies 147
Frost On The Pumpkin 91
Frosty Lime Pie 85
Frozen Chocolate Pie 83
Frozen Hawaiian Pie 82
Frozen Lemon Pie 87

Frozen Pies
  Baked Alaska.. 84
  Blueberry Alaska 84
  Choco Mint 82
  Chocolate 83
  Chocolate Mint..................................... 46
  Creamy Peanut Butter.......................... 88
  Frost On The Pumpkin 91
  Frosty Lime.. 85
  Fruit Alaska... 84
  Hawaiian 82
  Ice Cream 81
  Iced Lemonade..................................... 92
  Layered Fudge Frost............................ 81
  Lemon.. 87
  Mile High... 80
  Mud... 86
  Piña Colada 92
  Pink Velvet.. 42
Fruit Alaska.. 84
Fruit Pies
  Apple... 118
  Apple Cream...................................... 122
  Apple Raisin 102
  Blueberry 94
  Bumbleberry 127
  Canned Pear 102
  Concord Grape...................................... 95
  Coral Reef 100
  Cranapple 109
  Cranberry... 120
  Deep Apple... 96
  Dutch Apple.. 93
  Fresh Apricot..................................... 114
  Gooseberry... 96
  Grated Apple 117
  Mock Cherry 120
  Party Peach 97
  Peach... 98
  Pear 114
  Pear Streusel..................................... 121
  Pineapple.. 99
  Pineapple Cheese 116
  Plum... 104
  Plum Cream.. 103
  Plum Crumb.. 112
  Raisin... 98
  Raisin Cream...................................... 113
  Raisin Sour Cream 94
  Rhubarb... 118
  Rhubarb Cream.................................. 109
  Rhubarb Custard................................ 111
  Rhubarb Fluff..................................... 110
  Rhubarb Pineapple............................. 106
  Rhubarb Sour Cream 110
  Saskatoon... 94
  Snow.. 117
  Sour Cherry 104
  Sour Cream Apple.............................. 105
  Sour Cream Date 101

Sour Cream Peach................................... 122
Strawberry 112
Strawberry Pineapple.............................. 123
Strawberry Rhubarb 124
Upside Down Apple................................. 119
Winter 115

Gelatin Cherry Pie 51
Gingersnap Crust...................................... 91
Glazed Blueberry Pie 50
Glazed Cherry Pie 19
Gooseberry Pie 96
Graham Cracker Crust............................... 73
Graham Nut Crust 51
Grape Pie, Concord................................... 95
Grapefruit Chiffon Pie............................... 40
Grapenut Pie 138
Grasshopper Pie 42
Grated Apple Pie 117
Green Tomato Pie 136

Hot Water Pastry 139

Ice Cream Pie.. 81
Iced Lemonade Pie 92
Impossible Pie 56
Impossible Pies, See Crustless Pies
Impossible Pumpkin Pie............................. 59

Jam Tarts.. 146
Japanese Fruit Pie 8

Kentucky Derby Pie................................... 12
Key Lime Pie 44

Layered Fudge Frost.................................. 81
Lemon Angel Pie...................................... 129
Lemon Cheese 79
Lemon Cheese Tarts 79
Lemon Chess Pie 10
Lemon Chiffon Pie..................................... 46
Lemon Cream Pie 77
Lemon Meringue Pie 65
Lemon Pies
  Black Bottom Lemon 65
  Creamy 52
  Frozen.. 87
  Iced Lemonade...................................... 92
Lemon Sponge Pie..................................... 10
Lemonade Pie 37
Light Strawberry Pie 32
Lime Pies
  Creamy 44
  Key Lime.. 44
Lime Chiffon Pie 22
Lime Meringue Pie 65

Macadamia Nut Pie 74
Maids Of Honour 146
Maple Pie, Chilled 33

Maple Pecan Pie 30
Margarine Pastry 139
Meringue... 65
Meringue... 135
Meringue Crust Pies
   Angel.. 128
   Berry Angel... 131
   Brownie Angel 130
   Chocolate Angel 128
   Lemon Angel 129
Meringue, Two Step 79
Mile High Pie 80
Millionaire Pie 41
Mince Tarts 150
Mocha
   Chiffon, Chocolate 23
   Chocolate 32
   Mud.. 86
Mock Apple Pie 134
Mock Cherry Pie 120
Mock Pies
   Carrot... 137
   Eggnog 132
   Grapenut.. 138
   Green Tomato... 136
   Pecan Trix 132
   Sweet Potato 136
   Vinegar 135
   Zucchini 133
Mock Pumpkin Pie... 134
More Fried Pies 147
Mud Pie 86

No Crust Fudge Pie....................................... 58
Nutty Graham Cracker Crust 28
Nutty Pies
   Brownie.. 12
   Candy Pecan.. 14
   Chocolate Pecan 12
   Japanese Fruit....................................... 8
   Kentucky Derby 12
   Maple Pecan.. 30
   Osgood 11
   Pecan... 15
   Pecan Cheese.. 9
   Pumpkin Pecan 20
   Raisin Nut 16
   Turtle.. 13
   Upside Down Apple................................ 119

Old Time Pastry.. 142
Orange Chiffon Pie.. 39
Orange Juice Pastry...................................... 142
Orange Meringue Pie 69
Orange Mousse Pie 38
Osgood Pie... 11

Party Peach Pie.. 97

Pastry and Crusts
   Best Oil 141
   Chocolat Pie Shell 26
   Chocolate Cookie 29
   Chocolate Crisp 82
   Chocolate Graham 85
   Favorite 140
   Gingersnap.. 91
   Graham Cracker..................................... 73
   Graham Nut Crust 51
   Hot Water... 139
   Margarine 139
   Nutty Graham Cracker 28
   Old Time 142
   Peanut Butter... 138
   Puffy.. 141
   Short Nut 80
   Shortbread 24
   Vanilla Wafer... 87
Peach
   Party 97
   Sour Cream 122
Peach Ice Cream Pie 34
Peach Pie 98
Peanut Butter Pie, Creamy 88
Peanut Butter Cream Pie 66
Peanut Butter Crust....................................... 138
Pear Pie.. 114
Pear Pie, Canned 102
Pear Streusel Pie 121
Pecan
   Candy 14
   Pumpkin... 20
Pecan Cheese Pie... 9
Pecan Pie.. 15
Pecan Trix... 132
Piña Colada Pie... 92
Pineapple
   Cheese 43
   Cherry 28
   Cherry Pine.. 47
   Coral Reef 100
   Millionaire.. 41
   Rhubarb 106
   Strawberry 123
   Sweet... 56
Pineapple Cheese Pie.................................... 116
Pineapple Chiffon Pie..................................... 45
Pineapple Deluxe Pie 29
Pineapple Glory Pie 24
Pineapple Pie 99
Pineapple Wink Pie 20
Pink Velvet Pie 42
Plum Cream Pie 103
Plum Crumb Pie 112
Plum Pie 104
Puffy Pastry 141
Pumpkin Cheese Pie...................................... 76

Pumpkin Chiffon Pie 27
Pumpkin Pecan Pie 20
Pumpkin Pie 75
Pumpkin Pies
   Frost On The Pumpkin 91
   Impossible 59
Pumpkin Streusel Pie 68

Raisin Cream Pie 113
Raisin Nut Pie 16
Raisin Pie 98
Raisin Sour Cream Pie 94
Raspberry Citrus Pie 21
Raspberry Pies
   Berry Angel 131
Rhubarb, Strawberry 124
Rhubarb Chiffon Pie 38
Rhubarb Cream Pie 109
Rhubarb Custard Pie 111
Rhubarb Fluff Pie 110
Rhubarb Pie 118
Rhubarb Pineapple Pie 106
Rhubarb Sour Cream Pie 110

Saskatoon Pie 94
Sauces
   Blueberry 77
   Caramel 78
   Chocolate 81
   Custard 78
Shoofly Pie 8
Shortbread Crust 24
Short Nut Crust 80
Snow Pie 117
Sour Cherry Pie 104
Sour Cream
   Cocktail 37
   Lemon Cream 77
   Pineapple Wink 20
   Puffy Pastry 141
   Raisin 94
   Rhubarb 110
   Strawberry Cheese Tarts 145
Sour Cream Apple Pie 105
Sour Cream Chiffon Pie 55
Sour Cream Date Pie 101
Sour Cream Peach Pie 122
Sour Cream Pie 62
Sour Cream Tarts 62
Strawberry
   Fresh 40

Light 32
Strawberry Cheese Pie 31
Strawberry Cheese Tarts 145
Strawberry Pie 112
Strawberry Pie, Fresh 40
Strawberry Pineapple Pie 123
Strawberry Rhubarb Pie 124
Streusel Topping 105
Streusel Topping 121
Sugar Pie 75
Sweet Pineapple Pie 56
Sweet Potato Pie 136

Tarts
   Apricot 148
   Butter 150
   Butterscotch 149
   Chocolate 149
   Chocolate Fried Pies 147
   Cocojam 145
   Fried Pies 147
   Jam 146
   Lemon Cheese 79
   Maids Of Honour 146
   Mince 150
   More Fried Pies 147
   Sour Cream 62
   Strawberry Cheese 145
Tart Shells 140
Toppings
   Coffee 26
   Crumb 121
   Meringue 65
   Meringue 135
   Streusel 105
   Streusel 121
   Two Step Meringue 79
   Whipped Cream 30
Turtle Pie 13
Two Step Meringue 79

Upside Down Apple Pie 119

Vanilla Wafer Crust 87
Vinegar Pie 135

Watermelon Pie 49
Whipped Cream 30
Winter Pie 115

Zucchini Pie 133

COMPANY'S COMING
PUBLISHING LIMITED
BOX 8037, STATION "F"
EDMONTON, ALBERTA,
CANADA T6H 4N9

COOKBOOKS

SAVE $5.00 *Order any 2 cookbooks by mail at regular prices and SAVE $5.00 on every third cookbook per order.*

ENGLISH TITLE	QUANTITY	AMOUNT
(Hard Cover @ $17.95 each)		
JEAN PARÉ'S FAVORITES VOLUME ONE - 232 pages		
TITLE **(Soft Cover @ $10.95 each)**		
150 DELICIOUS SQUARES		
CASSEROLES		
MUFFINS & MORE		
SALADS		
APPETIZERS		
DESSERTS		
SOUPS & SANDWICHES		
HOLIDAY ENTERTAINING		
COOKIES		
VEGETABLES		
MAIN COURSES		
PASTA		
CAKES		
BARBECUES		
DINNERS OF THE WORLD		
LUNCHES		
PIES		
LIGHT RECIPES (April, '93)		
MICROWAVE COOKING (Sept., '93)		
TOTAL ENGLISH BOOKS (Carry total to next column)		$

FRENCH TITLE	QUANTITY	AMOUNT
(Soft Cover @ $10.95 each)		
150 DÉLICIEUX CARRÉS		
LES CASSEROLES		
MUFFINS ET PLUS		
LES DÎNERS		
LES BARBECUES		
LES TARTES		
DÉLICES DES FÊTES		
RECETTES LÉGÈRES (avril '93)		
LES SALADES (mai '93)		
LA CUISSON AU MICRO-ONDES (septembre '93)		
LES PÂTES (novembre '93)		
TOTAL COST OF FRENCH BOOKS		$
TOTAL COST OF ENGLISH BOOKS		$
TOTAL COST OF ALL BOOKS		$
LESS $5.00 for every third book per order		−
PLUS $1.50 postage & handling **PER BOOK**		+
SUB TOTAL		$
Canadian residents add GST #R101075620		+
TOTAL AMOUNT ENCLOSED		$

Please send the above cookbooks to the address on the reverse side of this coupon.

- **ORDERS OUTSIDE CANADA:**
  Must be paid in U.S. funds by cheque or money order drawn on Canadian or U.S. bank.

- *Prices subject to change without prior notice.*
- *Sorry, no C.O.D.'s*

- **MAKE CHEQUE OR MONEY ORDER PAYABLE TO:** *COMPANY'S COMING PUBLISHING LIMITED*

GIFT CARD MESSAGE

We will gladly enclose your personal message with cookbooks sent as gifts.

Company's Coming
COOKBOOKS

A GIFT FOR YOU

COOKBOOKS

I would like to order the Company's Coming Cookbooks listed on the reverse side of this coupon.

NAME _____
(PLEASE PRINT)

STREET _____

CITY _____ PROVINCE/STATE _____

POSTAL CODE/ZIP _____ PHONE (____) _____ - _____

GIFT GIVING – WE MAKE IT EASY...
...YOU MAKE IT DELICIOUS!

Let us help you with your gift giving! We will send cookbooks directly to the recipients of your choice if you give us their names and addresses. Be sure to specify the titles of the cookbooks you wish to send to each person.

Enclose a personal note or card for each gift or use our handy gift card below.

Company's Coming Cookbooks are the perfect gift for birthdays, bridal showers, baby showers, Mother's Day, Father's Day, graduation or any occasion...collect them all!

Don't forget to take advantage of the **$5.00 saving...buy any two Company's Coming Cookbooks by mail and save $5.00 on every third copy per order.**

GIFT CARD MESSAGE

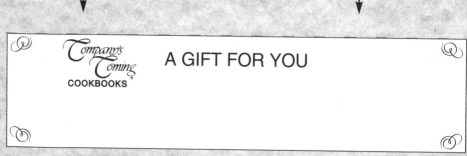

COOKBOOKS

COMPANY'S COMING
PUBLISHING LIMITED
BOX 8037, STATION "F"
EDMONTON, ALBERTA,
CANADA T6H 4N9

SAVE $5.00 *Order any 2 cookbooks by mail at regular prices and SAVE $5.00 on every third cookbook per order.*

ENGLISH TITLE	QUANTITY (Hard Cover @ $17.95 each)	AMOUNT
JEAN PARÉ'S FAVORITES VOLUME ONE - 232 pages		

TITLE	(Soft Cover @ $10.95 each)	
150 DELICIOUS SQUARES		
CASSEROLES		
MUFFINS & MORE		
SALADS		
APPETIZERS		
DESSERTS		
SOUPS & SANDWICHES		
HOLIDAY ENTERTAINING		
COOKIES		
VEGETABLES		
MAIN COURSES		
PASTA		
CAKES		
BARBECUES		
DINNERS OF THE WORLD		
LUNCHES		
PIES		
LIGHT RECIPES (April, '93)		
MICROWAVE COOKING (Sept., '93)		
TOTAL ENGLISH BOOKS (Carry total to next column)	$	

FRENCH TITLE	QUANTITY (Soft Cover @ $10.95 each)	AMOUNT
150 DÉLICIEUX CARRÉS		
LES CASSEROLES		
MUFFINS ET PLUS		
LES DÎNERS		
LES BARBECUES		
LES TARTES		
DÉLICES DES FÊTES		
RECETTES LÉGÈRES (avril '93)		
LES SALADES (mai '93)		
LA CUISSON AU MICRO-ONDES (septembre '93)		
LES PÂTES (novembre '93)		
TOTAL COST OF FRENCH BOOKS		$
TOTAL COST OF ENGLISH BOOKS		$
TOTAL COST OF ALL BOOKS		$
LESS $5.00 for every third book per order		−
PLUS $1.50 postage & handling **PER BOOK**		+
SUB TOTAL		$
Canadian residents add GST #R101075620		+
TOTAL AMOUNT ENCLOSED		$

Please send the above cookbooks to the address on the reverse side of this coupon.

- **ORDERS OUTSIDE CANADA:**
Must be paid in U.S. funds by cheque or money order drawn on Canadian or U.S. bank.

- *Prices subject to change without prior notice.*
- *Sorry, no C.O.D.'s*

- **MAKE CHEQUE OR MONEY ORDER PAYABLE TO:** *COMPANY'S COMING PUBLISHING LIMITED*

GIFT CARD MESSAGE
We will gladly enclose your personal message with cookbooks sent as gifts.

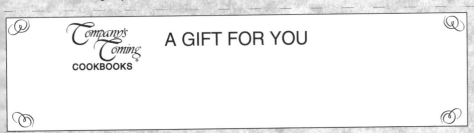

COOKBOOKS

A GIFT FOR YOU

COOKBOOKS

A NATIONAL **BEST SELLER**

I would like to order the Company's Coming Cookbooks listed on the reverse side of this coupon.

NAME _____
(PLEASE PRINT)

STREET _____

CITY _____ PROVINCE/STATE _____

POSTAL CODE/ZIP _____ PHONE ( ) - _____

GIFT GIVING – WE MAKE IT EASY...
...YOU MAKE IT DELICIOUS!

Let us help you with your gift giving! We will send cookbooks directly to the recipients of your choice if you give us their names and addresses. Be sure to specify the titles of the cookbooks you wish to send to each person.

Enclose a personal note or card for each gift or use our handy gift card below.

Company's Coming Cookbooks are the perfect gift for birthdays, bridal showers, baby showers, Mother's Day, Father's Day, graduation or any occasion...collect them all!

Don't forget to take advantage of the **$5.00 saving...buy any two Company's Coming Cookbooks by mail and save $5.00 on every third copy per order.**

GIFT CARD MESSAGE

▼   ▼

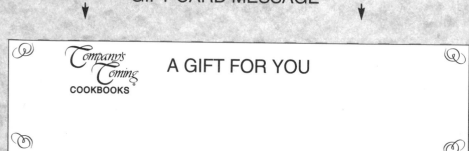

COOKBOOKS

A GIFT FOR YOU